AF584050

Luigi Maria Epicoco

Salt, Not Honey

For a faith that stings

Published in Australia by
Coventry Press
www.coventrypress.com.au
33 Scoresby Road Bayswater VIC 3153
an imprint of Freedom Publishing Books
www.freedompublishingbooks.com.au

ISBN 978-06-483-2332-7

Catalogue-in-Publication entry is available from the National Library of Australia http://catalogue.nla.gov.au

First published in Italy by
©2017 Edizioni San Paolo s,r.l.
Piazza Soncino 5 - 20092 Cinisello Balsamo (Milano) - ITALIA
www.edizionisanpaolo.it

Printed in Australia by Brougham Press

To Father Daniele Libanori, SJ
For all the 'salt' and time given.

Contents

Foreword

> 'Well, a man can't live on jam, and neither can a Christian society. Our Heavenly Father said mankind was the salt of the earth, son, not the honey. And our poor world's rather like old man Job, stretched out in all his filth, covered with ulcers and sores. Salt stings on an open wound, but saves you from gangrene.' (George Bernanos, *The Diary of a Country Priest*).

Were someone to ask us why it is worthwhile trying to become saints, our answer should follow along the lines of Bernanos: 'so as not to spoil or go bad.'

Our life is constantly on the brink of spoiling, but this is not a pessimistic thought. On the contrary it is a very optimistic view of things. Living things risk spoiling, things overflowing with life. Dead things, withered things are not at risk of going off because there is no life left in them, hence no risk. Blood flows from a living body. Sickness develops where there is life. A wound hurts because it afflicts a living body. Holiness is the attempt to keep life going, not let it go bad, not allow the excess of life to become the beginning of the end. This is why it is a mistake to think that holiness consists of a facile kind of 'do-goodery'. It is rather something that costs us some pain, just as salt makes us feel when we apply it to an open wound.

I myself had to go through a period in my life where holiness was mixed with a sugary notion that had little to do with my real life. I recall, when I was still a small boy, being taken to a number of vocation weekends with my other altar boy friends. Almost every evening we would watch slides together depicting the life of some saint or other. The rather unromantic rattle of the slides changing was masked by an audio-cassette recounting the life of the particular saint. And in case you think this is heading in the direction of a caustic critique of this kind of experience, I have to say that, on the contrary, I remember these stories with much nostalgia, since they nurtured an ever-growing desire in my heart to take faith in Christ seriously, because I was immersed in a world which, at the time, was accustomed to faith, the Faith, much like we grow accustomed to a particular song, or the ritual gesture of a wave when we greet a friend down the street. The problem was the imagined notion of holiness rather than the desire that was growing in my heart. For quite a while I thought that holiness was the romanticised view of reality, where the triumph of good vibes and smiles despite everything else, embodied and summed up what saints were about. The heroism of being good! Alas, I learned to my cost that holiness is a much more pressing issue. It is the heroism of remaining human despite life. And to remain human, at times we need to be strong, not good; shrewd, not naive; decisive, not submissive. Paradoxically, the disappointing colours in the slides brought me more convincingly closer to the saints whose story they were telling.

By some mysterious design of Providence, I have had occasion to meet many people, so many communities and ways of living Christianity. I have had the grace of spending time in the silence of monasteries, but also of immersing myself in the full-throated song of large gatherings. I have seen so many normal situations in parishes everywhere and have spoken with individuals who have had their lives changed by unimaginable events. What holds all these people together? Simply, that whatever way they live their life and faith, beneath it all is the common denominator of baptism, which has made us sons and daughters and given us the inner certainty of being loved, of being immersed in something whose underlying destiny is a good one, and knowing that love is the requirement for every life worthy of the name. In other words, faith, hope and charity. These are the three potentials received as gift in baptism, and we are called to express them whatever the circumstances of our life.

It is a serious undertaking because the quality of the rest of the world depends on the successful outcome of our adventure:

> You are the salt of the earth; but if salt has lost its taste, how can its saltiness be restored? It is no longer good for anything, but is thrown out and trampled under foot. You are the light of the world. A city built on a hill cannot be hid. No one after lighting a lamp puts it under the bushel basket, but on the lamp-stand, and it gives light to all in the house. In the same way let your light shine before others so that they may see your good works and give glory to your Father in heaven (Mt 5:13–16).

'So that they may see,' and have the urge to lift up their gaze, look upon Someone else.

The words which make up this book come from these encounters. While I have listened to many words, the ones I have written here have been prompted by the eyes of those who have stood before me. It would take too long to list every individual, community and experience involved. These pages are but a small sample. I am personally grateful to them all.

Luigi Maria Epicoco

Prologue

(The bare minimum)

As perhaps you might expect, before coming to the heart of our reflection I would like to say some things I consider essential for a more correct understanding of the pages that follow.

What is spiritual life? Spiritual life is not a technique, a set of rules or something we do. To be more precise, we should really see that our spiritual life is not so much what *we* do, because it is what the Spirit does within us. When people say they need to recover their spiritual life, it is as if they were saying that they need to be aware of what is happening to them, how the Holy Spirit is at work within them. Our primary contribution is 'to notice'.

When people take time out for their spiritual life they shouldn't spend it racking their brains, trying to extract some 'brilliant idea' for their life. In reality it is time taken to learn how to be in silence, and not simply to stop talking. It is time for listening.

Keeping quiet and being in silence are two radically different things: we can be quiet, keep silent, but the mind and heart might well be somewhere else rather than with the reality before us.

Instead, we can be in silence, listening fully to what is before us. This happens when we stand before something we love.

Silence is a way of fully seizing upon the present moment.

We are usually prepared to listen to someone around us when that person is a nice individual, we know they like us, and when we suspect they have something interesting to tell us. What, then, disposes us for silence is no mere command to 'be quiet!' but the fact that we have an urgent personal need to listen to something other than our own thoughts and emotions.

But if the spiritual life is what the Spirit does within us, we need to be careful not to confuse the spiritual life with the inner life. This latter is none other than all of our emotional, psychological, affective, rational set-up, our 'world within'. The inner life is our fully human capacity to perceive reality in an in-depth way and not simply for what it encompasses, its superficiality.

Everyone has an inner life as thus described. It is something we should always remind ourselves of and foster, because it is not tied to having or not having faith. The inner life is tied to our being human or not. It is the bare minimum for truly calling ourselves human. At the heart of the drama, the crisis we are going through, in my opinion, is the fact that even educational institutions like the school and culture in general have ceased teaching us the way of the inner life. In many cases it is actually literature, art, philosophy, and music, history that teach us the way of the inner life.

Yet, what we call the humanities seems to have been replaced by other priorities more to do with the marketplace. This lack of familiarity with the inner life makes us terribly superficial and, as a result, unhappy, and in many cases depressed.

Yet a Christian cannot be content with simply having an inner life, being content with this bare minimum. The Christian should dig deeper into this inner life to find the vein flowing deep within, with the waters of spiritual life, noting the life which is there but not dependent on their person: it is the life of the Spirit.

Giving ourselves the time, allowing ourselves silence, means refining the ability to notice the psychological movements within us, and knowing how to distinguish them from the spiritual ones. We also need to keep in mind that sometimes, psychological movements disguise themselves as spiritual movements. This happens when Jesus Christ is invented in our image especially through our needs: this is not Jesus of Nazareth, not the Son of God. It is then that silence, attention, the life of prayer, the Word above all, are like a filter that can help us sift what is spiritual from what is not. It is a trite example but it can fit the idea I would like to convey.

It is the same principle we use when we buy fruit, and touch or pinch it, so we can feel whether it is good or not. In the same way the spiritual life is a practical science. It teaches us an inner sense of touch so we can understand what comes from God and what simply comes out of our own story.

We make the error of simply continuing to interpret our feelings, and so catch the disease of fatalism ('If I feel this, then God wants to tell me…'; 'If this has happened then God wants…'). At times we get it right, but it is like getting up in the morning, checking the horoscope and thinking it is right. We all know the inconsistency of this kind of belief, because a horoscope tells us everything as well as its opposite. We are taken in by it every time. The truth is, that when you want it to tell you something, you let the horoscope confirm it, even believing it is God telling you, at times – that this is what you need. So we have to regain freedom from ourselves, from what we feel, from the anger we feel or the wound we have. We need to be aware, too, that while God does not need to make us suffer in order to tell us something, for sure, somewhere beneath our suffering, lies an argument that needs listening to, because God always fills what happens with meaning.

We need to understand prayer life as being emotionally involved in the life of Christ. It is an *affective involvement*.

This is a turning point, because usually our involvement in Christ's life is of the informative kind. We have so much information but we do not always allow ourselves to be involved to the point of feeling it, or truly believing in it all. The real nub of faith is that we take an interest in Christ's life in its entirety, intimately, and that we want to be involved with him in a much deeper way than just by simple reason; by involving all our other faculties, our whole being – not without reason, but with reason plus the rest. Until we manage to reach this turning point, and while we stay at just the purely rational, informative level, Jesus Christ's life is not a life that will change us.

We can consider what can happen these days when a boy falls in love with a girl. He immediately looks her up on social media. But can we describe his contentment at finding information on the girl, her virtual profile, as a relationship? He could say he is head over heels in love, that he knows so much about her, but the truth is that the relationship cannot only be knowledge of certain data: it has to become encounter, an exchange, dialogue, or in other words, a relationship. At times our Christianity is like this: we have accumulated so much information about Christ but that doesn't mean we have risked our life in a truly emotional, affective way.

The term that follows on from 'affective' is 'effective'.

So the process should be: from an informative to an affective life; from an affective life to an effective life, meaning real life.

We need faith to be real and not simply inwardly focused.

Conversion

Every time we put our 'spiritual zone' more resolutely and decisively at the centre of our life, it would be better to use that much misunderstood word 'conversion'. Very often, however, when we speak of conversion we give it moralistic overtones: people convert when they no longer commit evil. Not committing evil can be a consequence of conversion but it is not conversion in and for itself. The most serious evil in the Bible is not sin, nor is it unbelief: the most serious evil in the Bible is idolatry. *Conversion is getting rid of idolatry.*

Idolatry is our attempt to freeze God in a formula, an image, an idea, in something we have made of him to our own design. This is not in itself always negative because it is human to create our own view of things. But in the long run, certain crystallised images stall our journey, stop us from moving on. For example, it could happen that in our inner and spiritual life, our experiences produce certain images of God in us and we feel quite secure within these.

We codify them, develop and explore them, but without our realising it, these very images at times hinder, block our spiritual life.

So we need to go through the trauma of destroying them. We need to destroy the images of God we have created, while knowing that an image gives us certainty, makes us feel secure, and to be honest, we are all looking for security or certainty. 'You shall not make for yourself an idol, whether in the form of anything that is in heaven above, or that is on the earth beneath, or that is in the water under the earth' (Ex 20:4).

Christ is constantly asking us to embark on the uncertainty of a journey, removing everything that seems to us to be useful. This 'loss', this 'purification' is essential for us to be able to move on. Idolatry does not allow journeys, only illegal stopovers. We go nowhere with idolatry, we become static.

Thumbing through the Old Testament, and more exactly the history of the people of Israel, we immediately notice one tribe in particular. It is the priestly tribe, Levi's tribe, which has no rights to a plot of land. It has a right to inheritance but of a very special kind. The Lord tells Levi's tribe: 'I am your inheritance.' We understand better the inspired words of Psalm 16: 'The LORD is my chosen portion and my cup; you hold my lot.' (Ps 16:5). While everyone else has ground beneath them to stand on, the one who follows the Lord in the intimacy of the Levite, who can touch and transport the Ark, has no land on which to rest his feet. He has Him. It is He who is his ground. He has no human certainty like the others but does have God.

We could almost say that the true sign of the presence of God in our life resides in the fact that we have none of the human certainties the world suggests. Instead, very often we spend the vast majority of our life constantly, daily, extracting small certainties on which to build our days, our time, our existence.

The Holy Spirit does exactly the opposite: he loves us to such an extent that he constantly removes all kinds of certainty from us, because he wants to re-establish that very profound intimacy with God, given precisely through a sense of commitment to him, in him and with him. He wants us to touch the Ark, even before we touch ground.

When you lose the ground from under your feet, it means you are going somewhere. In order to journey there is a need to detach ourselves from the sure ground we are treading on.

Because idolatry means losing sight of God as the centre of our existence, it inevitably leads us to being always defensive, and inwardly this manifests as hardness of heart. Without our being aware of it, our heart paradoxically becomes stone in order to remain afloat. So what, then, is conversion? It is seeing these words come to pass: 'I will remove from your body the heart of stone and give you a heart of flesh' (Ezek 36:26). The Lord is the only one who can give us back a heart of flesh and purify us, free us from our idols. We need to return to having a heart which is risky because it is flesh, even if it is a nuisance to have such a heart. A heart of stone is better! A heart of flesh suffers, feels, is vulnerable, fragile, but not one of stone. No. Yet we cannot be happy with a heart of stone, only with a vulnerable heart of flesh. The only way we have for lowering our defences and accepting a heart of flesh in ourselves is to feel loved. This is the Lord's aim.

Do what you choose to do

'The wind blows where it chooses,' also a reference to the Spirit. It is sufficient to go to the third chapter of John's Gospel to note this, where it tells the story of a nocturnal disciple: Nicodemus. There is a very human reason why we can call Nicodemus a nocturnal disciple: he is afraid of judgement by others, afraid someone might judge his friendship with Christ badly. So, he shrewdly invites Christ to speak to him at night so no one can see him. This is very interesting, because Nicodemus is a Pharisee, part of the Temple, someone with certainties who lives by these certainties. He also lives by the formality his religion provides; he certainly has something to do with a religious current that does not look kindly on foreign influences on how to observe the Mosaic law. Yet despite having the outward certainties in the law and, considering this, the proper code for human, spiritual and moral reference, Nicodemus feels deeply fascinated by Jesus Christ, whom we could describe by contrast as anti-certainty.

Christ is a foreign body when compared to the attitude by which a devout Israelite understood faith and God. So then, how is it possible that we live by constructing certainties, roles, images around us and then feel deeply drawn to Christ, who tells us to leave behind everything in terms of formal and worldly certainties? We experience a kind of neurosis, schizophrenia: on the one hand we cling to things, and on the other we yearn to put out into the deep, navigate realms broader than the narrow ones our life is usually consumed by. It is the energy of the Spirit which constantly enkindles in us this need to put out into the deep. And, indeed, let me tell you it is a need to extend ourselves, broaden horizons, broaden the mind, the heart, our very humanity. In encountering Nicodemus we are facing up precisely to our own deepest neurosis. Nicodemus is the best image of what usually happens in our spiritual, our inner life. On the one hand, we want certainty, and on the other, we are dying to have experiences of things that remove us from security, from where we are fully in control of life. People born of the Spirit, who allow themselves to be led by the Spirit, lose control; it is the Spirit who is in control, and this makes us giddy and fearful at the same time. We know how to recognise a yearning of the kind, this breath of the Spirit within us. Initially, what happened to Nicodemus will also happen to us: we will be looking to find some compromise between our idea of things and this need, between our very human certainties and what the Spirit is asking of us.

While, on the one hand, we can find some room for our human power to give us a minimum of certainty, on the other, there is the Spirit in us saying: 'Let go of everything and trust in me.' So what are we trying to do? We don't want to let it all go, but nor do we want to disregard that voice; we look for a compromise, a nocturnal Christ. Converting ourselves means moving from night into light, renouncing our compromises which usually give us the illusion of having squared the circle by saying: 'On the one hand, I can keep my certainties, and on the other, listen to the Holy Spirit.' One cannot be a disciple of Christ by night alone. Nicodemus understands nothing of what Jesus told him. He is full of questions, but without ever untangling the skein of it all. Because, whoever seeks compromise with Jesus will never gain an in-depth understanding of his message and will misunderstand it. This is what heresy is, fundamentally; misunderstanding Christ's message, because we want to square it with certainties we do not wish to abandon. What is the theological term for certainties? They are idolatries.

Further on, we will take a good look at this mechanism, seeking to understand it in the stories of some particular biblical figures, like Abraham, for example. Even Isaac can become an idol for his father Abraham, who has to symbolically kill him, traumatically detach himself from him. Detachment from what we hold on to is always painful. There is no way out. It seems to be a fearful thing: the son of the promise, the son he always wanted, whom he has had and is enjoying, is the one he has to 'murder'. It seems as if this God asks horrible, cruel things of us. In reality, behind this apparent violence is the attempt to constantly give us back the freedom needed to be able to follow him; the freedom needed to be able to understand him, enter into a profound relationship with Christ, and hence with life itself and, as a consequence, with Isaac himself. The Gospel tells us:

> He came to Jesus by night and said to him, 'Rabbi, we know that you are a teacher who has come from God, for no one can do these signs that you do apart from the presence of God.' Jesus answered him, 'Very truly, I tell you, no one can see the kingdom of God without being born from above' (Jn 3:2-3).

The kingdom of God is not the result of discussions or reasoning, calculations, proposals, plans. The kingdom of God is the result of a vision that comes from being born from above.

To be able to see this kingdom of God, each of us must be re-converted. Put another way, we could also convince ourselves that the Lord is asking something of us – but it is not the Lord, it is our fear, or perhaps it is our frustrations, our insecurities disguised as God. What could be happening is what happens to certain men when they fall in love: it is not the woman they are looking at, but their fear of remaining single all their life. The first woman who comes along will give them children if they marry her. But in reality they have never got to know the woman. She has simply solved their fear of remaining single. A man of this kind has never really encountered the other, and has simply transferred his fear. The question is, can we be happy this way? No. Perhaps we can live a life without too many complications, but not presume to be happy with this way of satisfying ourselves. So, we need to be careful not to use religion, our projects, our desires, as a way of filling our void. The only thing we can possibly do is seek the kingdom of God, and to do this we need to be born from above, let ourselves be converted, be turned upside down: 'Nicodemus said to him, "How can anyone be born after having grown old?"' (Jn 3:4). The old age Nicodemus is speaking of is not years but the inescapable direction of life. It is the old age of someone who says: 'But I have always done it this way, how can I do the opposite? I have always been like this, I'm used to living like this; I was brought up this way.' How can people be born when they are old? Can they, perhaps, enter their mother's womb a second time and be born again? Who will give us another opportunity? An opportunity like we were given when we were twenty years old? Who can give us another chance like this? How can we be reborn, re-enter our mother's womb and be new again? It is another serious problem: we want great changes, but then, looking at ourselves and factoring in our humanity, we become aware that we do not have the wherewithal and opportunity to change, because we think that what the Lord is asking of us, he is asking us to do by our own efforts.

Instead, being born from above and being converted means understanding that all this is not something that relies on our capabilities. It is something only He can do. It is not something asked of our strength but of our ability to trust Him. This is humility. We have so often misunderstood this word, thinking humility is simply humiliation, a submissive, docile, meek and surrendering attitude. Humility, as the Word teaches us, is something very beautiful and serious. Humility means ceasing to trust in ourselves and beginning to confide only and exclusively in Him.

The humility asked of us is to trust in God alone, against everything and everyone, and especially against ourselves and our natural tendency to resign ourselves, to give up.

To understand the profound significance of this radical trust, perhaps we ought recall the story of Jairus, told in Mark's Gospel. Jairus has a daughter who is dying and goes to Jesus in desperation: 'My little daughter is at the point of death. Come home and cure her.' Jesus sets off toward the house, accompanying the father in his sorrow. But he is stopped by a woman who has been sick for more than a dozen years, and she too is desperate. In her desperation she thinks that if she can just touch Christ somehow, she will be healed. She touches him and is healed, but despite the crowd milling around him, Jesus obstinately wants to look the woman in the eye: 'Who touched me?' The disciples tell him: 'Everyone is touching you.' 'Who touched me?' He wants the woman who has been healed to relate to him, not simply be content with the healing, but build a personal relationship.

The time lost, however, due to this incident along the way, is fatal: Jairus' daughter dies: 'Why trouble the teacher any further? Your daughter is dead.' What can be more unavoidable than death? What is more certain than death? Nothing. Jesus looks at this man, this father who has lost everything, and tells him: '…only believe.' And they resume their journey home. Here is someone humble: Jairus. He has no more human certainties, nothing more he can trust in. It is all dead. And right at the moment when all seems lost, Jesus looks him in the eye and says: 'Only believe.'

This journey of humility, which is a *kenosis*, a descent, a journey of being stripped, actually ends up in the raising of the daughter who is given back to her father and mother. What was dead is given back life, reborn in a completely new way.

I believe each of us carries dead hopes within, buried expectations, maybe peacefully put to rest. But no matter how peaceful, hope without life is dead, and is expectation without anything to wait for. No matter how much peace we have made with our dead hopes, they remain dead. However, the Lord does not ask us to resign ourselves, he asks us to trust, and this is something quite different.

We have confused resignation with humility, with 'staying dead and content.' Some also say, 'This is God's will.' No, God's will is life. You see yourself as dead, you are dead, but from this moment begin to trust me! And it is beautiful how, at a certain point, we note that all the journey of death and failure is filled with meaning by the Lord who has brought us to a more radical conversion, as if he wants to tell us: 'It was the only way I could use to get you back.'

At times, we feel we are at the mercy of events. In Jesus' era, what perception would they have had of circumstances around them? Who seemed to be really in charge, holding their destiny in their hands – Rome? Caesar? Herod? Certainly not Providence or the grace of God. Yet, two thousand years later, what do we notice? That despite Rome seeming to be in charge forever, or Herod winning out, there was a plan of God's grace, making room for itself amid the violence, selfishness, all the tendency to death and these men wanting to be in charge. This should cheer us up considerably: despite our humanity, despite the many Herods, Caesars, the obstacles we carry within and which get in life's way, God's grace makes room for itself and makes progress, leading us to the point where we can say, as we sing at the Easter Vigil: 'O happy fault that earned so great, so glorious a Redeemer.'

How beautiful it will be one day, when we look back over our story and say: 'Just as well what happened happened.' But we suffered so much. Just as well! We lost everything. Just as well! This is what earns such a great Redeemer.

When everything is taken from us we are ready to receive him.

The loss is not something that only concerns Jesus Christ. The cross is the shape of our holiness, and we can't understand being on the cross unless we are stripped bare and nailed to something. This is what Jesus is telling Nicodemus, and Nicodemus replies, 'How can these things be?' 'What is born of the flesh is flesh,' Jesus says, ' and what is born of the Spirit is spirit. Do not be astonished that I said to you, "you must be born from above." The wind blows where it chooses, and you hear the sound of it, but you do not know where it comes from or where it goes. So it is with everyone who is born of the Spirit' (Jn 3:6–8).

I have no reply. I don't know where the Spirit is taking me. I don't know where he comes from or where he is going.

These pages will offer no answer to this. I only know how we can try to grasp hold of him, ride his wave and go in the direction his wind blows.

We have no answers, only directions. Spiritual life is never an answer. When spiritual life becomes an answer, it becomes an idolatry. Spiritual life is always a direction to take, with everything a journey can bring with it: precariousness, falls, getting hurt, getting lost.

But we are children of a God who knows us down to the last little detail and who has counted the hairs on our head, so are we not authorised to think that everything which is happening at the moment is perhaps doing so under his gaze, in the wave of grace guiding our life? How much peace comes from knowing this: we are not lost; we are loved down to the last detail. To show how he loves us Jesus says in the Gospel:

> Very truly, I tell you, we speak of what we know and testify to what we have seen; yet you do not receive our testimony. If I have told you about earthly things and you do not believe, how can you believe if I tell you about heavenly things? No one has ascended into heaven except the one who descended from heaven, the Son of Man. And just as Moses lifted up the serpent in the wilderness, so must the Son of Man be lifted up, that whoever believes in him may have eternal life. For God so loved the world that he gave his only Son, so that everyone who believes in him may not perish but have eternal life (Jn 3:11–16).

What gives us the strength to make this journey and even to set out on it? It is the love with which the Father has loved us, which is not a declaration of love made simply in words. To tell us that he loves us, the Father did not do so in words, but through his Son's flesh. We do not have the cloying words of a merciful God before us. The mercy of God the Father is concrete to the point of almost being cruel, because this mercy is his crucified Son. This is how he tells us that he loves us. And by fixing our gaze on the crucified Son we say with Paul: 'He who did not withhold his own Son, but gave him up for all of us, will he not with him also give us everything else?' (Rom 8:32).

It is from here that we must regain our hope and retake our journey once more. It is in the love of the Son that we find the strength to begin the journey, accept being converted, being reborn from above.

We must allow the Lord to destroy all our certainties and replace them with his kingdom. Him, not things. Him, not the Earth. Him, not the World. Him, not our plans. Him and him alone.

When Jesus regains this exclusivity, it then means we have resumed our spiritual life in a healthy way. Nicodemus would not understand that until he saw it with his very eyes, when he would lift his gaze and see this man crucified. There is a conversion in Nicodemus. He is a half-caste – not really a disciple, but nor is he the pure Pharisee or priest. When he converts, he finds the courage to do one thing for the Lord. He would do it in the light of the Lord, toward the end of Christ's whole story:

> After these things, Joseph of Arimathea, who was a disciple of Jesus, though a secret one because of his

> fear of the Jews, asked Pilate to let him take away the body of Jesus. Pilate gave him permission; so he came and removed his body. Nicodemus who had at first come to Jesus by night, also came bringing a mixture of myrrh and aloes weighing about a hundred pounds. They took the body of Jesus and wrapped it with the spices in linen cloths according to the burial custom of the Jews (Jn 19:38–40).

Nicodemus would find the courage to say openly, with a gesture, what he believes. He would certainly be ostracised for this, but 'those who do what is true come to the light, so that it may be clearly seen that their deeds have been done in God' (Jn 3:21).

There is a dynamic in this shift from night to day. There can be no true conversion until we leave behind the Nicodemus who is looking for compromise, until we unmask him and bring him into the light, and not just any light but the light of the crucified Son.

In the face of the Father's love, which is his crucified Son, each of us needs to be enlightened and say: 'Who do I truly belong to? Where do I really come from? Where am I really going?' These are the radical questions we normally think we already have answers for. But it is really not the case, because very often we ourselves try to be the answer. I am 'the name I have given myself.' I come from what I decide to accept of my history. I am going where I think I will be fulfilled according to my perspective on things. But the truth is that we know almost nothing 'except Jesus Christ, and him crucified' (cf. 1 Cor 2:2), as St Paul says, meaning we know nothing else except that before each of us, before every decision taken, before everything that has happened, there is a Love who has loved me by giving his life for me.

This is why we are trying to name our idolatries; turn on a light, allow this light to illuminate the very human mechanism, the Nicodemus we have all built up for ourselves.

So, let us try to bring out those compromises we have woven into our everyday without realising it, despite our Christian practice. We can become experts in Christian life but at the same time be impermeable to the Spirit's action. This is the most fearful thing: his presence can become impermeable for each of us. In this area the devil is truly diabolical. He gives us the sensation of being religious, allows us all our Christian practices but takes the Spirit from us. It is as if he were saying: 'Use Nicodemus' logic, look for compromise in everything.' A state of life like this can bring us a nasty surprise as told by Jesus in the Gospel:

> He said to them, 'Strive to enter through the narrow door; for many, I tell you, will try to enter and will not be able. When once the owner of the house has got up and shut the door, and you begin to stand outside and to knock at the door, saying, "Lord, open to us," then in reply he will say to you, "I do not know where you come from." Then you will being to say, "We ate and drank with you, and you taught in our streets," But he will say, "I do not know where you come from; go away from me, all you evil doers!"' (Lk 13:23–27).

It would certainly not be a nice thing to hear, at the end of our life: 'I do not know you, I have never seen you,' especially when we thought in our heart of hearts that we were of the very best religious kind. It would be traumatic.

It would not be God being ungrateful, but us missing in action before him.

We weren't there. We were caught up in our own religiosity; faith shaped our way. We were not where the Spirit's action was.

Listening in order to believe

We do good and commit evil according to our imagined view of things. Perhaps it represents the most decisive part of our inner being, because everything we do is always set out in a 'vision' each has of life. For example, if I have a negative view of what a foreigner is then I interpret everything foreign as something dangerous I need to protect myself from, ward off, get rid of.

The 'black man' who might have been part of our childhood stories sometimes becomes the real black man, the person of colour, the person unlike what is familiar to me, a different person. And if what is different is dangerous for me in my imagination, then the gestures I make will be guided by the vision I hold onto inwardly.

Each of us has an image of good and evil which guides our gestures, including moral ones. Conversion is first of all purifying this image, letting the Lord destroy it so it gives way not to an image but a presence. 'Their idols are silver and gold, the work of human hands. They have mouths but do not speak, eyes but do not see' says Psalm 115. We have something like this idol in us. It is like what we experience (fear, insecurity, expectations) but is not alive. It is an image. It reassures us, but it is not a presence. Presence is the opposite to image. Presence is absence of image, the presence of life instead. Perhaps this is the reason why the most important word in the Bible is not 'see' but 'listen.'

The first time God makes himself present in human life he does not do so visually but by word. He addresses a word to Abraham. I believe this is precisely the true antidote in any purification, the antidote against all forms of idolatry: the shift from the verb 'see' to the verb 'listen.'

Your whole life is about becoming an ear. Listening is the most decisive thing about us believers. Let us train ourselves to listen to the Word.

What does all this attention to the Word do for us? Why all this attention to singing, savouring, listening, if we do not do the same in life? If the God we listen to from the Prophetic Books, or from the Psalms, from Old or New Testament, is not with us in our garden, as we stand before a plant, even a tomato plant, then of what use is he, really? You might say that it would be less than reverent to go from liturgy, from the Word, to a tomato plant, but this is really what our problem is, the split we create between what we consider sacred and what we consider profane; between what happens in church, in the liturgy, and what happens in everyday life. If people are trained to listen daily and be aware of God's presence, then they will always be listening and noting it. They will do it in nature, with a brother or sister, faults included. Someone who lives by this listening hears the background sounds of God's presence even in ugly things, in the most contradictory events.

If it is true that God exists, he exists even in the pain and suffering of an earthquake or tragedy. We cannot say he is not there in that deep maelstrom of darkness and suffering. We cannot say he is present only where there is glory and light: 'If I ascend to heaven, you are there; if I make my bed in Sheol, you are there' (Ps 139:8). What could God have to do with Sheol? Yet 'Here you are' says the psalmist. There is no place not permeated by this Presence, but we can only see it by listening to it.

In reality, our eyes coincide with our capacity to listen. This profound obedience, this profound and radical listening is what we call discipleship.

We are disciples when we listen to his presence. When we are trained to do this, we become a bit like Elijah. Elijah sought to hear the Lord in the earthquake, in the wind, but he neither saw nor heard him. He felt oppressed, burdened by a great wish to die, there in the desert, overcome by a terrible depression immediately after having beaten the priests of Baal. This too is interesting: he wins but goes into a state of depression. It was enough for Queen Jezebel to threaten him for this to happen. This is quite special, because while it is true that the Lord had been with him during the struggle with the priests of Baal, and he had won, the Lord then let Elijah take things in hand. The Lord had not told him to massacre the priests, but overwhelmed by enthusiasm, Elijah had them all put to the sword, and paid dearly for his excessive zeal. Why? Fundamentally, what is depression? It is losing sight of the horizon of meaning. This horizon of meaning is replaced by a void, and then it seems nothing can make it worth while to go on living. Sometimes we can find ourselves in the desert with a great wish to die. This intent of Elijah's is not a simple prayer, not the spiritual life, no simple listening to the Lord. It was suicidal intent. And it is there, at the very heart of Elijah's depression, that the Lord speaks to him: 'If I make my bed in Sheol, you are there.' I like to think that this man, trained to listen, kept his ability to listen even in the depths of depression, his Sheol. He is so accustomed to listening that he keeps this attentive ability even when depressed. Yet it is not enough to be trained to listen or be accustomed to the things of God. The prophet Elijah would certainly have been better trained than we are at that, but it does not automatically mean we are spared from depression.

It can happen, at times, that we enter a netherworld (Sheol) we have not chosen nor wished for, and yet we find ourselves buried in such depths. What saves us is the ability to discern that God is not in the uproar, not in special effects, not in all the things that attract attention but, as the Scriptures say, 'in a sound of sheer silence' (cf. 1 Kings 19:12). In order to listen, we need to be in sheer silence. It is the noise of a gentle breeze.

When he hears this sound of silence, Elijah immediately understands he is in His presence and covers his face. What happens when he listens? A new beginning. Dear Elijah, the Lord is saying, you think that all is lost, but in reality I have my very faithful people and can take this whole story in hand once more:

> Then the Lord said to him, 'Go, return on your way to the wilderness of Damascus; when you arrive, you shall anoint Hazael as king over Aram. Also you shall anoint Jehu, Son of Nimshi as king over Israel; and you shall anoint Elisha, Son of Shapat of Abel-Meholah, as prophet in your place. Whoever escapes from the sword of Hazael, Jehu shall kill; and whoever escapes from the sword of Jehu, Elisha shall kill. Yet I will leave seven thousand in Israel, all the knees that have not bowed to Baal, and every mouth that has not kissed him' (1 Kings 19:15–18).

Elijah's time is over, but the Lord also wants to show him that the final word does not belong to Sheol, the netherworld, or to what his feelings of depression might suggest to him. There is a plan that goes beyond any depression we might experience. What is it that saves Elijah? Listening. Our ability to listen, this daily training, is very valuable because it keeps the only thing that can save us from idolatry, at the centre of things.

Why is it that monasteries seem to have all the good things? The best chocolate, beer, liqueurs, infusions, hand-crafted items? Because people who are trained to the Lord's presence, to serve him because they recognise him in what is sacred, and understands that the profane is equally sacred, do everything out of love, carefully, with dedication, passion, with relish, giving it everything. They look after something we normally consider to be ordinary, do so slowly, with appetite, putting all of themselves into it. When someone manages to do this it brings out the sacredness of the rest of creation, of a stone, a plant, a place, a book. These are normally profane realities, but when they are loved, worked on and experienced by someone trained to recognise the Lord's presence, they are all transformed by this presence.

This does not mean we believe a table contains God; we are not pantheists. But we do believe that this table is an opportunity for loving God. God is not here within it, but I use this table as an opportunity to tell God: 'I love you.' This is why I live well, do things well, look after things well, clean things well. I do not recognise any divinity in these things, but I understand that everything is an opportunity for loving him.

Who is the brother or sister living near me? An opportunity for loving God. In this sense my brother or sister are necessary for us. Not essential but necessary, which is different. Only Jesus Christ is essential; everything that exists in our life is necessary. When I have brought all these things of his back into communication, then that Presence I experience in one part of my life spreads to the rest of my life and tells him: 'Everything speaks and cries out about you.'

Feeling and thinking

Now I would like to move on. What does this purification of our imagined view of things do for us? What helps free us from idolatry? Two things, fundamentally, should clear some space in us. We can sum them up in two words: 'feeling' and 'thinking.'

I have borrowed these two words, these two verbs, from St Paul. At a certain point he writes to the Philippians: 'Let the same mind be in you that was in Christ Jesus' (Phil 2:5). Then, in the First Letter to the Corinthians, he continues: 'For we have the mind of Christ' (1 Cor 2:16).

What does it all mean? That being in relationship with Christ should not simply produce a purification from idols in us, take away an image to give us a presence; this presence, truthfully speaking, transforms us radically. We begin to feel life as Jesus Christ feels it, our thoughts and our feelings enter into a very deep harmony with his.

Devotion to the Sacred Heart developed in the 19th Century, especially through the work of the Jesuits. When we love someone, our heart begins to beat in harmony with that person. Deep harmony is created between ourselves and the loved one. It always end up with the two becoming like each other.

This is the proof that we are in his presence; at a certain point, without seeking it, with no particular effort, we begin to become like Jesus.

This terrified me for a while, and gave rise to not a few problems. I said to myself: if I need to make room for Christ in me, as St Paul put it, 'until Christ is formed in you' (Gal 4:19), then where is my freedom? Or worse still, where am I, if Christ's thinking, Christ's feeling emerges in me? Where am I in all this? Do I not also have a right to exist? Will my thoughts no longer have their own dignity? My feelings too? What purpose does freedom have? I believe that a kind of battle goes on inside us, ever dying to ourselves, because the verb 'to die' is hardly a romantic one. But I believe there is a great misunderstanding when we think of dying as the Gospel understands it, since Christian dying is not about disappearing. Christian dying is about making room. When we die 'to ourselves' we do not disappear 'as ourselves,' our individuality is not over. When we die to ourselves, it is as if we have accepted making room for someone else in us. The Lord gave us an extraordinarily eloquent example in a story from the Old Testament, a beautiful but complicated story. It is the story of Moses.

It will help to throw some light for a moment on this man's life so we can more broadly understand the sense in which making room for Christ in no way takes away our individuality, our uniqueness, our being who we are. But let's get to the story. While Moses was happily tending to Jethro's flock, by now far from Egypt, and thinking he had built a new life for himself a long way from the troubles he had left behind, he encounters the Lord. The Lord manifests himself to him through a rather interesting event:

> Moses was keeping the flock of his father-in-law Jethro, the priest of Midian; he led his flock beyond the wilderness and came to Horeb, the mountain of God. There the angel of the Lord appeared to him in a flame of fire out of a bush; he looked and the bush was blazing yet it was not consumed. Then Moses said, 'I must turn aside and look at this great sight, and see why the bush is not burned up.' When the Lord saw that he had turned aside to see, God called to him out of the bush, 'Moses, Moses!' And he said, 'Here I am.' Then he said, 'Come no closer! Remove the sandals from your feet, for the place on which you are standing is holy ground,' He said further, 'I am the God of your fathers, the God of Abraham, the God of Isaac, and the God of Jacob.' And Moses hid his face, for he was afraid to look at God (Ex 3: 1–6).

What is this burning bush? It is something that attracts Moses' attention and makes him curious, since he sees a bush burning, but not being consumed. The fire, in order to be fire, should consume combustible material. What strikes Moses, is that there is fire but it does not consume the dry bush beneath. He is not surprised by the fire itself: these things happen in the desert where surely phenomena of auto-combustion were generally widespread.

What makes him curious is seeing a flame, and seeing the bush intact at the same time. To exist, a flame should consume, but in this case it does not consume; it adds. What does this flame add? Light and warmth. Who is God? He is someone who adds something to our life, not someone who takes something away from it. He does not need to exist at our expense. God's presence is not a battery, not something that needs to consume us in order to survive. He is precisely the flame of the burning bush in us, a flame that burns and does not consume, which adds warmth and light, but not at our expense. Dying to ourselves means allowing God to add something, to make room within our individuality. He puts a little more light and warmth of his presence into our cold and worthless individuality. Christ's thoughts and feelings are not a replacement for us but an addition, an expansion of our heart and mind. I continue to have my character, my story, my wounds, my sensitivity, but theology tells us that we are called to conform ourselves to Christ.

What does it mean to conform ourselves? There is a scene in a film by Liliana Cavani, *Francesco* (1989) that can help us. In the sequence which describes Francis of Assisi's conversion, there is this significant moment: Francis, who has taken refuge in the vicinity of San Damiano, climbs up into the semi-destroyed church and picks up pieces of the ancient crucifix, the famous San Damiano Crucifix, and embraces it. If we were to freeze the frame at this point we would notice that for a few moments, while he was embracing the cross, Francis' face was superimposed exactly over the face on the crucifix. He has a halo around him, as if he himself were the Christ. He had 'conformed,' which in practical terms means 'he had taken the same form.' Here is the meaning: we have the same form as Christ while remaining who we are in substance. We are the substance but the form is Christ, which is the more correct way of describing the substance. Christ works this change within us. We become in his image but we remain ourselves, profoundly who we are. It is a mystery that leaves us speechless. It is what we could call a spiritual transformation. Just as in the Eucharist there comes a moment in which what you see is bread, what you taste is bread, but in reality it is Christ (transubstantiation/change of substance leaving the form intact). In the spiritual life the exact opposite takes place: we remain who we are in substance but the form is Christ's. All of our spiritual life is learning to extend our arms like Christ did on the Cross. It is learning to take his form. Those open arms of Christ on the Cross say so much about what our spiritual life should be, because when we think of our spiritual life, what comes to mind is a kind of concentration, a kind of turning in on ourselves. But instead, conforming ourselves to Christ is extending our arms. Open arms speak of acceptance, embrace, openness. And this openness is so great that it can never be transformed into closure. For the sake of security, his hands are nailed, so the idea of closing them never occurs to us. What are so often our wounds, our nails, are reassurances the Lord gives us, so we do not close our arms. Paul had understood this when at a certain point he said:

> Therefore to keep me from being too elated, a thorn was given me in the flesh, a messenger of Satan to torment me, to keep me from being too elated. Three times I appealed to the Lord about this, that it would leave me, but he said to me,' My grace is sufficient for you, for power is made perfect in weakness.' So, I will boast all the more gladly of my weaknesses so that the power of Christ may dwell in me. Therefore I am content with weaknesses, insults, hardships, persecutions, and calamities for the sake of Christ, for whenever I am weak, then I am strong (2 Cor 12:7–10).

I believe there is a plan of grace even for our sins. That is, God guides even our fragility which tends toward evil. He guides it in such a way that it can contribute to our good: 'We know that all things work together for good for those who love God, who are called according to his purpose' (Rom 8:28).

There are times when we need to experience failure and defeat, a 'no'. Life does not educate us only when everything is going well. There is a time when it is good for life to go badly, and it is precisely because it goes badly that it helps us to re-dimension ourselves, or rather to discover our true dimensions. Each of us, I believe, has failures where we feel drained. The Lord also has a plan for these failures. They are not blotches, but God's capacity to have everything contribute to our good.

The image of the burning bush, of being conformed to Christ, is what best makes us understand what it means for us to make room for the light and warmth of his presence. In existential terms it means making room for Christ's 'feeling' and 'thinking. Even vocation is conformation to Christ by taking a particular path: loving a woman, loving children, loving a ministry, living certain situations in a contemplative way. We all have a piece of real life in which we are trained in this holiness, in being conformed to Christ. In the gospel, Jesus translates this conformation to Christ thus: 'No one has greater love than this, to lay down one's life for one's friends' (Jn 15:13). The maturity of every spiritual life is expressed in these terms: I am mature to the extent that I succeed in giving my life. If I am a father, I must learn to give my life for my children every day. I must learn to give my life for my brothers and sisters every day. I must learn to give my life for the Church every day. I must learn to give my life for someone who is away from the Church and whom the Lord places before me.

If we re-read the parable of the Good Samaritan without immediately falling into moral application, we could say that perhaps the priest and Levite we have mistreated for centuries in our preaching and explanations, were not completely wrong. In their thinking, in their mentality, their main responsibility was to be busy about their sacred matters, matters of law, the Temple. The serious problem is that they do not notice that giving your life is not something you can determine, when and how you want, nor is it enough to always refer to the general rule of your calling. Giving your life is something God determines, when and how he wants. And if he has put you on the road where a man is dying, he decides at that moment that it is a priority. Are we capable of recognising this presence, accepting that God does as he wishes, that the Spirit blows where he wills? I believe that people who go looking for martyrdom are not clear about what the gospel is saying when it teaches loving to the extent of giving our life. Martyrs do not seek this: they encounter it. One doesn't go to one's death smiling, but with all the drama of someone who would like to keep living, yet if the choice is between living to save one's life and dying for a just cause, then one chooses to die out of love.

I believe that every now and again, we are all caught up in this enthusiasm in which we want to give our lives, but our real problem is that we almost never sign a blank cheque as to how. St Anthony of Padua comes to mind. As a religious he was fascinated by the charism of Francis, the poor man from Assisi. He sees a small group of Franciscans go out and return as martyrs. He wants to do the same, wants to also die as a martyr in the land of Islam. But while trying to do so, he ends up shipwrecked in Sicily. The Lord speaks to Anthony through these events: 'No, I do not need you to lose your head for me there. I need you to die elsewhere, for you to give your life elsewhere.' Thus this man from Lisbon would die in Padua.

Having the availability to give our life is not for us to decide. We have to leave it to the Lord to arrange. We mature to the extent that we leave it to him, let ourselves be guided by him, allow him to tell us: 'Now is the moment.'

During the time I spent in Paris, in 2010, I had the opportunity to see the film/documentary called *Of God's and Men* (2010). The film is a reconstruction of the martyrdom of a community of eight Trappist monks living in Tibhirine in Algeria. It was 1996, and the news event was disturbing, due to the monks' obstinate determination not to leave the people, the majority of whom were Muslims, themselves going through the torment of war and increasing violence.

> At a time when many were thinking of Islam as the enemy, the gesture of someone allowing himself to be slaughtered (like the Lamb in the apocalypse that is slaughtered) while loving his executioner, is the extreme rejection of the logic of enmity, and the only act that can bring an end to the chain of vendetta and revenge. It is Christianity's serious case, its hard core: it is the cross (Enzo Bianchi).

I was especially struck by the ending of this account, the concluding sequences. What were the final moments of these brothers of ours like? There was no TV camera, no fictitious idea, no incense; there were no candles and hymns; there would have been all the drama, the precariousness of what took place. One cannot choose the manner of one's death.

But it continues to be a rather urgent reminder that our availability is not for dying but for 'giving our life'. I would like to spend a moment with this distinction. The Lord does not ask us to die but to give our lives, because it is life we are talking about, even if it culminates in martyrdom. What is it that is the foundation, for example, in living together in marriage, a family, a community? It is knowing that despite our faults, our human side, despite my brother's or sister's weaknesses, despite the human uncertainty or the situation, we are all growing in spiritual life, and I am aware that the people beside me would give their life for me, not out of duty but out of love! 'I desire mercy, not sacrifice' (Mt 9:13). This means that at times we do everything out of duty. We even look after our brothers and sisters out of duty. We do everything we have to do out of duty. We respect others out of duty. We prepare excellent dinners out of duty. But the Lord is asking us to do all this out of love, not out of duty. They are all occasions when we can give our life, meaning our love. 'I give my life! I am ready to die for you' must be seen from the perspective of love.

What is the purpose of duty? St Paul comes to our aid: 'Therefore the law was our disciplinarian until Christ came, so that we might be justified by faith' (Gal 3:24). Think of a sapling which has a stake next to it when it is small; when the tree gets bigger it no longer needs the stake. For a while it is needed, to keep it straight. But if a tree were tied to a stake for all of its life the tree would fail. At a certain point, the tree must take the direction it is given. Does duty help? Of course it helps! But it is not our life's purpose. Our life's purpose is to learn to love, not learn to do our duty.

Can love be bought? Do you think that good works can buy love? We very often think so, since it is the mentality we have received. Without our realising it, our educators begin forming us through reward and punishment. 'If you behave well, I will give you something'; 'If you do well at school I will give you a reward; but if you behave badly mum will no longer love you.' It is awful how we are psychologically wounded by statements of this kind. It stamps a business logic on us which is not the logic of love. My mother still loves me even if I do not do my chores, even if I behave badly, because love is either freely offered or it does us harm, because it is not love. Inevitably, when we have experienced love of this kind, we carry it into our relationship with God. We think we can manage God like this, as a transaction, through duty. We control our whole spiritual life by trying to understand how this business is going. So, how would we be if at the end of our life we present ourselves before him and lay it all out on the table? Maybe he would sweep it all off with his hand, look us in the eye with his love, true love, and tell us: 'I only want to know one thing: are you happy?' 'Lord, I wasn't ready for this question, but I have done my duty.' And he would say to us: 'My will was for you to be happy, not for you to simply do your duty.'

What is hell in this instance? It is when anger and bitterness overcome us and we say, 'I could have been happy or at least have lived.'

When we lose sight of this love, as Christ teaches us through his 'feeling' and 'thinking', his mindset and way of life, it all gets complicated, everything becomes hell, even if we don't notice it is hell. So, if it is true that we always end up becoming like those we love, then we should become like Christ. And to become like Christ, we need to conform ourselves to him in love.

There is an interesting passage in the Book of Revelation:

> To the angel of the church in Ephesus write: These are the words of him who holds the seven stars in his right hand, who walks among the seven golden lamp-stands. I know your works, your toil and your patient endurance. I know that you cannot tolerate evildoers; you have tested those who claim to be apostles but are not and have found them to be false. I also know that you are endeavouring patiently and bearing up for the sake of my name, and that you have not grown weary. But I have this against you that you have abandoned the love you had at first (Rev 2:1–4).

You no longer love me as you loved me at the beginning. However you are persevering, you hate evil-doers, but the most important ingredient of all is love. Is there any of the love we had when we began our journey? Is there anything left of the love we had when we fell in love and imagined all kinds of things, and then realised that life is so cruelly real and not ideal? We use the word 'ideal' because it is different from the real. Are there any ideal people? No. If if they are ideal, why are there only real people? How do we become holy? By getting angry, because the person beside us is not the ideal wife or husband or child, or friend? No. By loving what is real. The truth is that we have to make peace with the real and not pretend that others will become ideal. What is love? It is love for what is real, not ideal. Christ did not put an ideal love in our heart, but a real love.

The love of the Son is an incarnate love: ‘The Word became flesh,’ real, ‘and lived among us’ (cf. Jn 1:14).

With the logic of the Incarnation, we no longer seek an ideal but something real: Christ is the flesh of our brothers and sisters. They are the prolongation of Christ over the time and space of history.

1

Faith

(Or why knowing he loves me is better than knowing he exists)

Before dealing with the subject of the three theological virtues, I would like to offer a necessary theological preamble. When we speak of faith, hope and charity, we say that we find ourselves before theological virtues. The obscure word 'theological' describing 'virtue' means something very simple: these virtues come from God and are not an endowment of ours, not what characteristically equips us to be human beings. Yet, in life's normal practice, it sometimes happens that we enter a vicious circle of guilt produced precisely by faith, hope and charity. It all comes about because, without our being aware of it, we think faith, hope and charity are our human efforts; and since mostly we do not manage to live the dynamic of these three gifts fully, we feel we have failed, we feel guilty.

As we have just said, by theological virtues we mean a gift, and not just any gift, but a gift from heaven itself. In truth, no one is capable of faith or hope or charity unaided. At best, humanly speaking, we are capable of trust, which is something different to faith. We are capable of optimism, which is different from hope, and we are capable of good, which is a different matter to charity. Now, it is obvious that human attitudes should correspond to the theological gifts of faith, hope and charity, but human attitudes alone do not suffice.

Our trust in life is not enough to respond to everything that life so often presents us with. At times we need something more: this 'more' is faith.

It is not enough to have an optimistic view of things to always remain on our feet. We need something more, something that places us within a more extended horizon of meaning, something higher, and this is hope.

To be happy, it is not enough for us to be good. We need a greater, more profound charity that releases us from the human way of the *quid pro quo*, replacing it, instead, with the divine way of gift, hence the theological virtue of charity.

This is why, when we see that we do not have these three gifts, instead of feeling bad and guilty, we should do the simplest thing in the world: ask for them.

I often hear it said: 'Father, I am of the view that I have no faith.' 'Ask for it' I reply. 'But I think I do not have the hope to tackle what I have been given to live.' 'Ask for it!' 'I don't know how to love.' 'Ask for charity!' We fail to notice that the vast majority of important things in our spiritual life are a gift, and gift is only accepted through the logic of a child who goes to his mother and says: 'I need…'

What is the worst illness that can strike us in our spiritual life? Self-sufficiency, thinking we need no one; thinking that we need to grow to the extent of being embarrassed at receiving help from anyone, including God.

Spiritual maturity is quite the opposite. It is understanding that before God we are dependent. It is an essential, structural dependence for us. Jesus offers us a comparison to help us understand this: 'I am the vine, you are the branches. Those who abide in me, and I in them, bear much fruit, because apart from me you can do nothing' (Jn 15:5). Now, if a branch at a certain point wants to elevate itself to the dignity of being a trunk, it follows that from then on this presumption, this self-sufficiency it shows, will lead to its demise.

The freedom the Lord gains for us, is a freedom that occurs within a relationship. The world teaches us that we are only free when we have no need of anyone. Our faith teaches us that we are only free when we build relationships that render us free. Perfection is not in solitude; if solitude were perfection, our God would be one. End of story. Our God is One and Three. We are made in his image and likeness. What does that mean? That our perfection is not in solitude but in a 'trinity', a relationship. When we recover this relationship then our perfection emerges.

Not self-sufficiency but rapport, relationship. This is spiritual maturity.

Not solitude, but relationship.

We receive that which helps us, that which enables us to live, in this relationship. Let me offer a culinary example which might not be high theology but I hope it gives the idea: let us think of our life as being like preparing a minestrone. In fact it is made up of many different kinds of vegetables or, in other words, so many different experiences: our family, ourselves, our vocation, or decisions, what happens to us, what we have endured.

It is like a whole collection of vegetables. However, there is something, an ingredient which combines the lot, and it is salt. Salt gives flavour. What does it do in practice? It binds all the ingredients together. We are no longer faced with a collection of vegetables but a single dish, bound together by something you don't see but as you drink it, you know it is there. Here, then, is faith, which is something never seen but we notice it when eating, living.

We could say that faith always has something to do with experience. If there is faith then all the components of our life are combined, are in dialogue with each other such that they form a unity, not just a mixture of ingredients juxtaposed and undigested. Something good to eat. When we lack faith we have no valid reason in our life to make it worth the effort. Here is why, at some point, our life becomes unbearable, because we no longer succeed in squaring the circle, can no longer hold all the internal contradictions together. We tell ourselves that we are condemned to being unhappy because our life is too imperfect to be able to contain happiness. By now, we have been through experiences that have marked us to such an extent that we can no longer hope to be happy, because to be happy we feel we would need one, two, three, four, five things we no longer have. We have lost them. Yet is this really the case? Our happiness never really depends on life in itself, never depends on what is or is not in our life, but on how it is all held together. This is a profound inner change, a decisive basic awareness: it is not what is in our life that makes us more or less happy, but how it is held together. This creates happiness or not. Happiness always manifests as a sense of completeness, feeling our life to be something truly alive.

Instead, we feel we are lagging behind a bit, somewhat confounded, maybe in the right place but at the wrong moment, and we constantly experience the drama of not feeling loved or recognised. Happiness is the sense of fulfilment, letting ourselves be reached by a Love which tells us: *'This is my Son, the Beloved, with whom I am well pleased'* (Mt 3:17). These are the words the Father addresses to Jesus while the Baptist is immersing him in the waters of the Jordan. It is a declaration of love for every human being, because we are all baptised in Christ Jesus. Eternal life is allowing ourselves to be reached by God who says: 'You are loved, I have placed my trust in you.'

When people tell you: 'you are loved,' they are making you belong. We all need to belong, and only trust brings out the potential of our humanity in us. Not duty, not judgement, but trust. The greatest charity we can do for a person is the charity of trust. God trusts us.

If we thumb through the gospel, we note that when Jesus has to explain the logic of the end days, and the kingdom of God, he uses many images of a very similar kind: he speaks of lessees: 'Someone had a vineyard then leased it out and went away; he had a house and entrusted it to his servants and went away to another country.' At first sight it could look like exploitation: 'I have a vineyard. I'll get you to work on it, then I'll come back and want the fruits.' Instead, the truth is something other than this: this giving, then leaving, is an act of trust. Someone who gives you the keys of the house, then goes away, is someone who trusts you. Our God leaves us the keys of the house and tells us: 'You are not the owner but I am treating you as if you were a child of mine and I am trusting you.' This is why it would be possible for me to kill my brother, but no bolt of lightning would strike me down at that moment. Our freedom is real, not a pretence. Our freedom is not like when we get our licence, with the driving instructor seated beside us with dual controls to intervene at the last moment. How convenient it would be to be able to say: 'If I make a mistake the Lord will apply the brake.' No, it doesn't work like that. Our freedom is real to the extent that we can crash and hurt ourselves. It is real to the extent that we can be lost, even lost forever. Love could not exist without true freedom. And if what makes us complete is love, then love demands freedom.

This is why, in the history of the Church, the idea that hell does not exist has often been considered attractive, or that if it does exist then it is empty. But that would be a contradiction of the logic of love. If hell does not exist, then nor does love, because we would not be free. Love is an omnipotent God who hands himself over to us to the extent that he can be rejected forever. He takes that risk!

What is it that disturbs us in the faith? It is the fact that God exists, that by definition he needs nothing, yet despite this, he foolishly places himself in need of each of us. This is something we will never understand: how can it be possible for him to need nothing and at a certain point break this self-sufficiency to introduce us into his plan. Perhaps God needs my praises? No. 'You have no need of our praise, yet our thanksgiving is itself your gift, since our praises add nothing to your greatness but profit us for salvation' as we say in the liturgy. The love God has for us is a mystery beyond our comprehension.

Let me open a brief philosophical parenthesis: the word 'comprehension' is like an embrace: *com*-prehend, take in an embrace. 'Incomprehensible' means it cannot be grasped. But something you cannot grasp does not mean you cannot know it. To know it you have to extend your arms, that is, not wrap it in incomprehension but leave your arms wide open as in contemplation. And what is contemplation? It is relinquishing the effort to comprehend so we can remain constantly open before something which cannot be taken in but which I have an experience of just the same. Only contemplation can save us in this relationship with the Mystery.

We are somewhat a casualty of the Enlightenment culture. This is a little bit like a childish fault we carry with us: only what I experience exists; only what I can understand and measure by reason. There is an endless number of things in life we cannot understand, yet they exist. It is a mistake to elevate our head to being the absolute measure of things. If there is a truly decisive step in our lives, including for those without faith, it is contemplation of the Mystery, meaning we remain continuously open to something greater than us.

With this preamble, we can allow ourselves some help from our ancestor in faith, the father of all monotheisms, someone who to a degree binds even very different religious families together: Abraham.

Abraham is not only the father of Israel's faith, but also of ours as Christians. Islam also looks upon him as a father. We say that all three monotheistic religions recognise Abraham's fatherhood. But why is Abraham really important? Because it was to him that God first addressed his Word.

It is interesting to reflect on the fact that the first words God addresses to man, to his man called Abraham, is '*lekh lekha*':

> Now the Lord said to Abram: 'Go from [*Lekh lekha*] your country and your kindred and your father's house to the land that I will show you (Gen 12:1).

The literal translation of the expression '*lekh lekha*' is 'go toward yourself.' Thus Abraham becomes the ancestor of a twofold movement: one which is real, horizontal, because in real terms he leaves his father's house and sets out on a journey. And at the same time he becomes the ancestor of the spiritual life because the spiritual life is going toward ourselves, re-entering ourselves.

There is a journey which takes place outside, and one which takes place inside us. This has always been clear in our Faith tradition, to the point where for millennia we have gone on pilgrimages. What are pilgrimages? Why do people go to Santiago de Compostela? Why do they go on foot to some shrine? Why does the Via Francigena exist? Why does all Europe head to Rome? What use is a pilgrimage?

At certain times, we need to do externally what we must do in the intimacy of ourselves. That is, everything we do externally symbolises a journey we are making within. What we do outwardly helps us to do it inwardly. So, of what value should a pilgrim's way be? Not simply to take to the road, but to be converted. This way, the road becomes the manner by which I can return to myself inwardly. The road means tiredness, but also acceptance; it is ascent but also descent; it hurts our feet, but it is also finding relief; it is feeling hungry, but also feeling replenished. All the experiences we have on a journey, on pilgrimage, have an inward effect. Abraham is the first to enter into himself when he sets forth on an outward journey.

The entire history of salvation is a movement, a journey. The people of Israel never seemed to pause on their journey. It is perpetual motion. The choice of this people created a movement that cannot stop, just as the spiritual life cannot stop. We could even be two hundred years old, but our spiritual life would not stop. There is never a point at which we reach our permanent centre of gravity. If you observe a tight-rope walker on a rope ,you see he sways a little to the right and left. Were he to stay still he would fall. The same happens in our spiritual life. It does not stop, because we have achieved awareness, or a state of being that carries us forward. On the contrary, it is our consistent learning about the journey, learning to balance, that carries us forward.

We could also say that faith, as Abraham teaches us, is learning to depart, to set out on a journey. How do we do this? By abandoning some certainties. Faith continuously asks us to let go of certainties. If we can call certainty an idolatry, the idol we have created for ourselves, then faith is constantly leaving our homeland and setting out on a journey. To where? We do not know — it will be to where he points us. God does not say to Abraham 'Go there' in any precise way. He gives him no explanation, just an indication. The first response to this word addressed to mankind is Abraham's trust in direction. Faith is a direction, not an explanation. Faith does not provide explanations for a mother who has lost her son, and if we were to risk responding to the drama of a mother who loses her son, we would be blaspheming. Faith does not furnish explanations; only guidance in that sorrow. The question is, what road do we take in this suffering? Roads rather than responses. Jesus experiences his whole life like this. Faith is always an experience, a journey. It is a direction amid darkness, at times also in light, but it is always a road we need to travel.

This business of the road is so important, that over the centuries, the Church has understood that even a lifetime is not enough to reach the Promised Land, the reason why we have the extra time of Purgatory. It is like extra time on the journey given us, because we are returning home. It is a further direction despite our death. How clever is God's mercy in constantly inventing means and opportunities for getting back home!

The real departure point is when we leave — leave a certainty behind, allow the Lord to detach us from where we have paused, to set us on the journey once more. Whatever he asks of us outwardly, the Lord would always like to happen for us inwardly. If the distance we travel outwardly has no inner correspondence, we will not manage to stay upright. At times the journey corresponds to an illness we have to go through. The Lord asks us to leave the solid ground of our health and set out on the shaky ground of our illness. If that illness does not produce depth, insight in us, we will not deal with it. Instead of it being an opportunity to return home, to become saints, it becomes an occasion for condemning ourselves. Everything that happens outwardly is always *lekh lekha*, a journey inward toward our true selves. This is the first point.

The second point is an apparently nasty joke God plays on Abraham. He fills his heart with desire for a son, but in reality denies him that wish.

We could say that Abraham experiences this desire as martyrdom. What does this mean? What could a man like Abraham want? A family, children, descendants.

God fills his heart with a desire, because it is always God who fills our heart with desires. None of us invents desires, it is God who does this for us. However, the same God who filled Abraham's heart with the desire for fatherhood, has him go through the drama of infertility. How is that possible? How come God puts something in my heart, then in real terms denies it? I believe that sooner or later each of us experiences a paradox of this kind. But what strikes me most is what St Paul says:

> So I find it to be a law that when I want to do what is good, evil lies close at hand. For I delight in the law of God in my inmost self, but I see in my members another law at war with the law of my mind, making me captive to the law of sin that dwells in my members (Rom 7:21–23).

The desire for holiness is so great in me, and at the same time there is evidence of my failures, my sins, which say exactly the opposite to what I bear in my heart. This sets up an inner tension: between our desires and their realisation.

This is a most important characteristic of faith, because the martyrdom that comes to us from this desire placed in our hearts is what purifies us. Why does God wait before realising his promise? Why deny Abraham this promise in reality? It would be quite presumptuous on our part to answer this question, also because not even the Scriptures tell us why he waits. However, we can guess that there is a logic behind this waiting. The desire, indeed the martyrdom of desire, digs a hole like a well in us, an empty space. It is the space in which we can truly welcome God's promise. The denial of what we want very often prepares us to accept the promise more decisively and with greater awareness.

Hence, a Christian should be constantly practised at waiting. What does it mean to wait? Waiting means learning to make room for the promise God has placed in my heart. And what does it mean to learn to make room? It means allowing what we are waiting for to help us establish some priorities, to say: 'This is what I want and I want it with all my being. This is the most important thing I want.' Perhaps we should ask ourselves: what is our most important desire, the thing we await with most trepidation? Because that desire defines us. It is our identity.

The serious problem is remembering that this martyrdom of desire serves to purify us. From what? From what we imagine this promise to be, because God is forever failing what we imagine things to be — yet he always keeps his promise.

Think of a mother expecting a child: what does she do over those nine months? She imagines what that child will be like: 'Will it be like me? My husband? Will the child have blue eyes, brown eyes? Will it be a boy, a girl? Will it be good, etc.? Without being aware of it, she is designing her child, creating an imaginary picture. That view is destroyed when she gives birth. When the child is born it never coincides with the image, with what the mother imagined. Inevitably, when we have a promise in our heart, it is as if we were expecting a child and we begin to imagine something of the promise, how it should turn out. Yet when the Lord carries out his promise, it completely disappoints what we had in mind. But its realisation is the only way a promise is kept. It is God who places the desire for a child in Abraham's heart, but it is not up to Abraham to know who the child will be or when he or she will arrive.

Like us, Abraham suffers from impatience, and at a certain point reasons like other spiritual people when they employ a bit of common sense and shrewdness; 'If the Lord has placed this promise in my heart but in reality he is denying me of it, perhaps he wants me to seek a compromise, some fully human way of realising it. Why did I not think of it earlier? Perhaps this is exactly what the Lord is asking of me; perhaps for this promise of his to be realised it means I have to get to work somehow to find a solution. What can I do? I will have a child by Hagar, my slave-girl, and the baby to be born will be the realisation of the promise.' Ishmael was the result of a very human compromise in which Abraham, who wants to wait no longer, finds his own strategy to realise the promise. 'Lord, this was what you meant wasn't it? Look what I have done. It is Ishmael my son.' No, he is not the son of the promise, because God never asks us to devise human strategies to realise things; he asks us to trust in him against all hope, every situation, contradiction. ' I have a wife who is barren and what do you tell me? That I will have a son, indeed that my descendants will be as numerous as the stars in the heavens and the sand on the seashore. There is something here that is not working.' 'Yes, your faith is not working. Do you trust me?' 'Lord, I have more trust in my wife's barren womb.' Here is the lack of faith, trusting more in the limitations than in God's omnipotence.

This is the martyrdom of desire, the martyrdom of the promise the Lord places in our heart. We constantly experience limitations and God asks us: 'Who do you believe, the limitations or me?' This is where our faith comes into play. Abraham believed him for so long, but at some point he said: 'We will act as if I believe you but I will also find a way of overcoming the limitations in a human way.' No. Abraham sins, persuaded by a family system, among other things. But then, we know God will keep His promise, will keep it and give this man a son, Isaac, in his old age. Isaac is the son of the promise.

How great will the joy be after waiting a lifetime for something and finally receiving it? As great as the astonishment in saying: 'It's not possible.' At times we are so accustomed, so trained to disappointment and evil that when something good comes along we say: 'It is an illusion.' Evil and darkness are certain, but light a little less so. Something of the kind also happens in Abraham's life. It is like when we ask people, 'How's it going?' and they reply, 'Well, let me tell you quietly that things are going well.' We are so accustomed to the dark that when light comes we are afraid it is an illusion, or that someone will take it from us. Abraham too suffers from this. The illness that strikes Abraham is called possessiveness. It is a human reaction, very human, in seeing things realised that he had desired for so long and which had also been denied him for so long. When something is given to us, at times our reaction, other than joy, is one of possession. We want it all for ourselves. This is because in reality we have an enormous fear that someone might take it from us, or wake us from the dream.

Just as the flame burns the bush but does not consume, adds light and warmth to it, but not to the detriment of the dry bush beneath it, so in the same way, God's gifts are an addition which leaves us profoundly free. We should think of our life as falling into water and not knowing how to swim. By our efforts alone we will not manage to stay afloat and will need outside help, someone to throw us a lifejacket from a boat. Now it is obvious that the lifejacket can save our life, but unless we grab hold of it we will not automatically be saved. Faith is not a grapple that grabs us and pulls us out of the water. It is precisely a lifejacket tossed into the sea of life. It is up to us to employ all the human strategies to enable us to use that gift. We can understand, then, how we cannot feel safe simply because we have the gift of faith. The serious question is, are we also able to use it? Because we can have it and not use it.

I believe, then, that what the Word is suggesting to us is to understand that a human attitude, a human correspondence must go with the gift of faith. Faith has its demands.

In looking at the figure of Abraham, we have already seen how faith is about leaving our home territory, leaving behind our certitudes and setting out on a journey. Faith, not as a response but a direction, faith as an inner journey because everything the Lord gives us in our outward living must have a corresponding inward action. It if does not have this inner correspondence, everything outside does not work because it lacks depth.

At the same time, faith is the planting of a promise which the Lord places in our heart. As with Abraham, it means experiencing the martyrdom of desire: God places a promise in our heart. This promise is very often denied in reality, but a kind of maturity, a purification, comes from this struggle. God destroys the image we have created of the promise for ourselves, our expectations, our fictitious idea, whatever are we waiting for, but he does keep his promise, bringing about its true substance.

In the life of each of us there is always a unique name. The realisation of a promise always coincides with a unique name, that is, with something concrete.

One day, in our heart, we head the Lord calling us to something, a deeper intimacy, a love, a greater love, a different love. But it was all too vague until it became the unique name of a specific vocation, in a specific community, the name of a man or woman, or the name of a specific place, with specific brothers or sisters. The Lord always gives us an Isaac with a unique name. Not just any son, but Isaac. It would be interesting for us to understand or succeed in giving a unique name to the Isaac in our life. Who is Isaac? The son of the promise? The promise always kept, realised — or is it late in coming? Because faith is always a struggle. Yet by definition Isaac is the response to the desire, to the promise placed in Abraham's heart.

We should add, however, that Isaac is also the cause of the greatest temptation Abraham experiences: the temptation to possessiveness.

Give him to me!

We were saying earlier that at certain times we are so accustomed to bad news, effort, struggle, emptiness, that when good news turns up we are afraid, just as happens in one account in Mark's Gospel:

> When evening came, the boat was out on the sea, and he was alone on the land. When he saw that they were straining at the oars against an adverse wind, he came towards them early in the morning, walking on the sea. He intended to pass them by, but when they saw him walking on the sea, they thought it was a ghost and cried out: for they all saw him and were terrified. But immediately he spoke to them and said, 'Take heart, it is I; do not be afraid.' Then he got into the boat with them and the wind ceased. And they were utterly astounded for they did not understand about the loaves, but their hearts were hardened (Mk 6:47–2).

The disciples were crossing this lake in a storm, and Jesus goes to meet them. It should be re-assuring to see him walking on the waters and coming toward them to help them. Instead they cry out that it is a ghost! It is interesting to see how the first reaction of the disciples to Jesus trying to help them is to cry out in fear. We really are very particular. But the gospel recounts these episodes not to make us feel too strange. When the Lord responds to our being in difficulty, very often our reaction is one of fear. It seems almost inevitable even though we are very good people much taken up by prayer, contemplation. We are still human and our humanness always preserves some common traits.

Certainly, Abraham was a good person, devout and trustworthy, but despite this he is afraid of losing Isaac. This is where possessiveness comes from. The truth is we are not bad, not initially at least. Most of the mistaken things in our life come from fear. Possessiveness comes from the fear of losing something.

The issue of possessiveness is tied strictly to chastity. When we think of chastity, perhaps we think only and exclusively of physical sexual deeds. By definition, chastity is freedom from possession, not simply a physical and sexual-emotional thing. 'Called to chastity' means being free from possession of which physicality and sexuality are only a part, perhaps the extreme part, the more outward side.

There is a basic problem with chastity in our life. We have a skewed relationship with things and individuals, at times even with God himself. We lack chastity with God, perhaps because we want to possess him. Chastity is the call to be free with regard to this attempt to grab hold of things, to be able to possess them. But why do we want to grab hold of things possessively? Because we are afraid of losing them. We know that when we experience something beautiful we want it to stay forever, because beautiful things remind us of him, true things, good things remind us of him. So we grasp whatever reminds us of him possessively.

How does God help Abraham free himself from this temptation to possess in regard to Isaac? By asking just one thing of him:

> After these things, God tested Abraham. He said to him, 'Abraham!' And he said, 'Here I am.' He said, 'Take your son, your only son Isaac whom you love, and go to the land of Moriah, and offer him there as a burnt offering on one of the mountains that I shall show you.' So Abraham rose early in the morning, saddled his donkey and took two of his young men with him, and his son Isaac; he cut the wood for the burnt offering, and set out and went to the place in the distance that God had shown him. On the third day, Abraham looked up and saw the place far away. Then Abraham said to his young men, 'Stay here with the donkey; the boy and I will go over there; we will worship and then we will come back to you.'
>
> Abraham took the wood of the burnt offering and laid it on his son Isaac, and he himself carried the fire and the knife. So the two of them walked on together. Isaac said to his father Abraham, 'Father!' And he said, 'Here I am my son.' He said, 'The fire and the wood are here, but where is the lamb for a burnt offering?' Abraham said, 'God himself will provide the lamb for a burnt offering, my son.' So the two of them walked on together.
>
> When they came to the place that God had shown him, Abraham built an altar there and laid the wood in

> order. He bound his son Isaac and laid him on the altar, on top of the wood (Gen 22:1–9).

The Word of God is so very discreet in dealing with Abraham's psychological state. It does not tell us of Abraham's reaction. But I believe we all have a right to imagine how a father would react to such an absurd request. I am absolutely convinced that for parents, the greatest sacrifice is not their own life but the life of the child. I would also be ready to give up my life, but not my child's, which is much more precious than mine. I am always very moved by this, because thinking of this mystery I can understand better how much greater is the love of the Trinity. The most precious thing the Father can have is not his own life but the life of his Son. God the Father sacrifices his Son out of love for us. In qualitative terms, God's sorrow is much greater than that of anyone who just gives up their own life, because the Father's love is a love ready to give up his own Son out of love for me: 'In this is love, not that we loved God but that he loved us and sent his Son to be the atoning sacrifice for our sins' (1 Jn 4:10).

It is something that completely surpasses our ability to think about it. To free Abraham from possessiveness, God asked him to give Isaac back. In this silence, which not even we should fill with conjecture, there are many things we might be thinking, but we do not know exactly what could have been going through Abraham's mind and heart. We are in the midst of that silence; that is where our struggle is. It is a silence in which one could be allowed to say: 'Lord, I have followed you until now. It took you a while but in the end you gave me my son. But what sort of game are we playing now? Why are you asking me to sacrifice the thing

I want most? I could just take my son and go, go and hide. He is not someone I want to give you. Lord, your request is absurd.' Instead, Abraham obeys this command. It is not a sudden thing. There is a ritual, a liturgy, a journey, a way to go between the request and the ascent up the mountain where his son will be sacrificed. But this journey, this trek, is made up of silences. Not lies, but measured words: 'Isaac said to his father Abraham, "Father!"and he said, "Here I am my son." He said, "The fire and the wood are here, but where is the lamb for a burnt offering?" Abraham said, "God himself will provide the lamb for a burnt offering, my son."'

There is something in this story that throws me into a profound crisis. If Abraham is ready to sacrifice his son, why is God asking this of him? What is the difference between him and any other religious fanatic? The world is full of people who kill other people, thinking they are offering worship to God. Is this the example Abraham leaves us? Mere religious fanaticism? How can one go against such a simple, common sense thing as a father's love? How can we go against our very nature which tells us to protect the fruit of our own blood? Over how many centuries have we said that Abraham is our father in faith, is truly God's friend – because he behaved like a religious fanatic? He is ready to kill his son because God asks him to? Well then, I do not accept such a simplistic interpretation of this story. In this case it could not be any kind of example for us. To the contrary, it would be precisely the negation of what Christ asks of us in the Gospel.

Instead, I believe this apparently absurd story opens up a completely different view of faith within us.

What is faith? Faith is not simply believing that God exists. That is too little. Faith is believing He loves me. Taken this way, our perception of the story changes completely. Abraham is convinced that God loves him; he believes in God's love. He believes in it even when commands seem to contrast with this love. His is an act of faith in the love of this God, not the absurd execution of a command such as to kill his son. In his heart he knows this is irrational, but he does not know yet how God will resolve the contradiction. He trusts in the fact that God himself will resolve the absurdity of a situation of this kind. This is why he tells Isaac: '*Deus providebit*,' 'God will provide.' It is as if to say, 'My son, I do not know how we will get out of this, but I am certain God will pull us out of it.' Here is the revolutionary bit: Abraham is our father in faith because before all others he believes in the love of this Father, who is God. And even if everything is saying the opposite, he believes in this love against everything and everyone. Not even for an instant does the idea develop that God could permit such a thing, but he does not know what lies behind the command. Yet he knows he must obey what is happening to him, knowing God will resolve his problem. '*Deus providebit*.'

When the Letter to the Romans says of Abraham that he was 'hoping against hope' it fundamentally means he believed in God's love against everything and everyone rather than that he carried out God's command contrary to any logic. Here, I believe, is a very subtle but decisive line of demarcation in each of our lives. We are not people of faith, people of God, when we blindly obey what faith asks of us, but when we believe totally in God's love. We are not executors of commands but children.

Inevitably, this has existential implications for the rest of our faith life. Why is such a dramatic journey necessary? Why this sacrifice of Isaac, this taking seriously a God who says: 'Give him to me'? Because it is the only way Abraham can truly live his love for Isaac freely. Finally he can look Isaac in the face, can look at this son of his because he is no longer his possession. He has no more fear of losing him. God faced Abraham with his worst fear, losing his son, in order to heal this fear.

We all know that Isaac prefigures Christ. But the real difference lies in the fact that Isaac's sacrifice was suspended, Christ's not so. If we can describe Abraham's as an inner drama, the Father's drama takes place in the events themselves, in reality. This is why Christ brings about salvation for all, because in his sacrifice we are healed of every root of evil, fear and non-meaning. The trial Abraham endures, one so many of us often experience, is faced up to and conquered by Christ who takes the consequences of this trial upon himself. He struggles in our place. He loses in our place and because of this, conquers for each of us.

Now, if it is true that we all experience a problem with chastity because we experience a problem with possessiveness where things and people are concerned, and that the first root of possessiveness is the fear of losing the beautiful things we encounter and experience, then God is the one who frees us through faith from the dictatorship of possession. He calls us to chastity by asking us to believe more in his love than in our perception of things.

If we were to experience the requests the Lord makes of us in life as commands to carry out, we would be fanatics. If we were to accept celibacy or fidelity or honesty or giving freely, simply as the execution of commands, we would merely be soldiers with no other meaning. We accept something because we believe in His love, and that is radically different. 'Out of love for you I am ready to give you this.' It is no longer absurd when everything is re-read in the logic of love. This is often the missing piece for us. Everything becomes absurd when you forget that God loves you over and above everything and anyone, and that you must never doubt this love, even when everything else is urging you to do so.

Obstinacy that prays

> Jesus left that place and went away to the district of Tyre and Sidon. Just then a Canaanite woman from that region came out and stated shouting, 'Have mercy on me, Lord, Son of David; my daughter is tormented by a demon.' But he did not answer her at all. And his disciples came and urged him, saying 'Send her away for she keeps shouting after us.' He answered, 'I was sent only to the lost sheep of the house of Israel.' But she came and knelt before him, saying, 'Lord, help me,' He answered, 'It is not fair to take the children's food and throw it to the dogs.' She said, 'Yes, Lord, yet even the dogs eat the crumbs that fall from their masters' table.' Then Jesus answered her. 'Woman, great is your faith! Let it be done for you as you wish.' And her daughter was healed instantly (Mt 15:21–28).

When we are confronted with the bare, raw Word, we need to let ourselves be scandalised by it. This is one of the passages in which the Gospel's effect is exactly that, scandal. But let's go to the passage itself and see what is happening.

There is a woman, a desperate mother. She comes to Jesus not out of faith but probably out of desperation. We very often turn to God out of desperation, that is, we remember him when we need him. We should be very sincere in saying that more often than not, it is not our faith which brings us to God, but adverse circumstances.

I challenge anyone who remains indifferent before a mother's desperation. It is a desperate mother who goes to Jesus to say: 'My daughter is tormented by a demon.' 'But he did not answer her at all.' That much should at least be shocking, and as we gradually reflect on this silence, a feeling of confusion and anger mounts in us. It is okay for us to begin thinking: 'You are desperate, you are suffering, your child is dying. You go to God, appeal to Jesus and by way of an answer he says nothing.' At times we see heaven this way, as total indifference in our regard. At times it is an experience we have with our prayer. It is called 'the feeling of absence.' It is not really absence, but you feel it that way. You pray and you have the feeling that God does not even look your way and you were wasting your time going there. The truth is that the gospel is describing for us what this woman sees, not what Jesus is. The disciples arrive and they pretend to teach Jesus to act like Jesus: 'Send her away [other translations say 'Listen to her!'], for she keeps shouting after us.' In other words, 'She makes us look bad… What would it cost you? She is a desperate mother.' But Jesus increases the stakes: 'No, because I was not sent to her but to the lost sheep of the house of Israel.' So, he adds rejection to the feeling of absence. It really is too much. After rejection, why hang around? Instead, the woman obstinately stays put. It can happen that each of us feels God is keeping silent. Psalm 28 describes this experience thus: 'To you, O LORD, I call; my rock, do not refuse to hear me, for if you are silent to me, I shall be like those who go down to the Pit.' At times we also feel rejection added to absence: 'O LORD, why do you cast me off? Why do you hide your face from me?' (Ps 88:15). This woman, with her story, is telling us that Jesus exists and is involved with someone, but she is excluded from the group of those he is involved with. Happiness exists, but I am excluded from it. Grace exists but I am outside Grace. Good exists but I am left out. This is even worse, because if neither good nor happiness were to exist, at least there would be a minimum of justice for everyone. Instead no. The other person is listened to, is involved in good, but me, no. 'For you are the God in whom I take refuge; why have you cast me off? Why must I walk about mournfully because of the oppression of the enemy?' (Ps 43:2).

This psalm might sound like blasphemy, yet at times we feel this way, our spiritual life and prayer make us feel rejected.

What is to be done in these cases? Stay put, like this woman.

First of all, there is the movement from desperation to faith: 'But she came and knelt before him, saying, "Lord, help me."'

Desperation made her follow Jesus. At a certain point she places herself before him. Here is faith, when from behind you come to the front, look him in the face. We understand this more clearly in the gospel episode which tells about the woman with a haemorrhage. This woman thinks: 'If I could just touch the hem of his cloak I would be healed.' And in fact she touches Jesus' cloak and is healed. The story could end here, but no: Jesus stops and asks who touched him. Peter replies that they all touched him because the crowd is pressing around, but Jesus continues looking around to see who touched him. Because just encountering Christ's grace is too little; too little just to couch his cloak; too little to use God to do me a favour. This is not faith. Faith is eye contact with Jesus, building a personal rapport with him; not with his grace but with him, his person. Instead, our Christianity is very often the Christianity of the cloak and almost never arrives at Jesus' face. Many of us think we go to Church because we want grace, and not because we want to meet the person of Christ. Yet our true vocation as baptised individuals is to succeed in bringing ourselves and others from the cloak to the face, from the fringe to Christ, who dies out of a desire to encounter us personally. One day that woman, looking back over her story, will think that it was actually thanks to that illness that in the end she came to look Jesus in the eye. If she had been happy with grace alone she would have been cured, but not saved, because we are saved only when we meet Jesus Christ and not simply his grace.

At times, however, we are not interested in Jesus Christ. He is useful, but that's as far as it goes. The Canaanite woman makes the shift from *Jesus is useful to me because I am desperate,* to building a relationship with him. Due to this desperation she goes in front of him, kneels before him. That is interesting, because if you have experienced indifference and rejection in prayer, yet you stayed with it, you know that from then on your faith increased, as it did for the woman. This woman became simply a hand open before Jesus: 'Lord, help me.' In my little experience of faith I can claim that the further we advance in the spiritual life the fewer our words in prayer. The woman knows she has no need to explain her daughter's medical record, no need to convince Jesus of anything. She herself became her prayer: 'Lord, help me.' It is all there. Will Jesus finally listen to her? No. Jesus replies: 'It is not fair to take the children's food and throw it to the dogs.'

This seems quite over the top! How could Jesus possibly say something of the kind. Yet, this is the Word of God.

I feel you are not interested, you have rejected me, I feel you are treating me like a dog.

Sometimes in prayer, we do feel like dogs, thrown away. We would like to run, clear out. Then we feel sick when we come to pray because this feeling of rejection comes to mind. This is the perception we have: feeling like dogs. Yet right at the height of this dramatic experience, the woman makes her profession of faith: 'Yes Lord, yet even the dogs eat the crumbs that fall from their master's table.'

You are right, but I am staying put. Even knowing how worthless I am I know there is something for me.

'Woman, great is your faith! Let it be done for you as you wish.' Only in very few cases does Jesus lavish a compliment of the kind: for Nathaniel, for this woman, and for the Roman centurion. Rarely does Jesus liberally bestow compliments on the people he meets. *Woman, great is your faith*. To Nathaniel: 'Here is truly an Israelite in whom there is no deceit' (cf. Jn 1:47); to the centurion: 'Truly, I tell you, in no one in Israel have I found such faith' (cf. Mt 8:10).

What is faith, then? It is knowing how to remain at prayer even when our feelings and reasoning tell us to stop.

When we learn this kind of prayer, we no longer go to pray because 'it makes us feel good' but because we are like this Canaanite woman. We are people who experience ourselves as outsiders. Somehow, we too are Canaanites and have tremendous need of Christ. *You are necessary to us, Lord, the centre of everything*. When he is necessary he becomes the most essential part. It is no longer he who adjusts to us but we who are led to a very profound inner change. The change is that we come there desperate and leave with faith, a faith that gains its wish: 'Let it be done for you as you wish.'

If we think of the saints, those who perhaps worked too many miracles in their lifetime, we can immediately note their constant precision in saying they were not the authors of those miracles. The people did not understand immediately, and asked themselves how it was possible that the Lord acted so abundantly in a person's life. But the truth is, that when you empty yourself, it is the Lord who fills you, he who acts.

Sometimes, when we feel worthless, yet we have the faith to remain at our post just the same, we become very fruitful, because Christ did this too: he saved us through the Cross. It is through the Cross, not preaching or miracles, that he saved us. Every time we are in the same situation of being crucified we become like him, fruitful, and also able to channel his salvation.

This is what humility is. Humility is staying put when our emotional and rational side tells us to go.

Faith urges us to this point because it wants to teach us one very important thing: that we are not our emotions, not our thoughts, though we are convinced that we coincide with our emotions and thoughts. This is why we think spontaneously of leaving. At times, faith brings us to the point of emotionally and rationally experiencing a lack of interest on God's part, and it is there that we face the struggle to stay put, regardless. If you do stay, at a certain point you feel a split within. You understand that you are not what you experience and think, but are someone who stays put against all expectation. We could almost say that you are what you choose to be, not what you feel or think. I believe it is the cruellest struggle of faith. To explain it, Jesus tells us in the gospel: 'If any want to become my followers, let them deny themselves.' That is, go against themselves, go against what their emotional and rational set-up is telling them. 'Take up your cross and follow me' (cf. Lk 9:23). The experience of faith is an experience of going against oneself, learning to stay when reason and emotion are telling us, 'No, get out of here, there is no one here. No one loves you, you are not interested in anyone here. You can pray but no one speaks to you. It is a God who makes you feel like a dog.' Humility is the highest way of practising courage — the courage not to leave but to stay put.

In my pastoral experience I see that most people, when they approach a life of prayer, confuse it with their emotional state. For example, they come to pray because they feel something. This is not all bad; at times it can be the beginning, and we do feel good. It is bad when people feel they have lost their faith and no longer pray because they no longer feel anything. They have confused faith with an emotional state. Faith, and the experience of the spiritual life and prayer, go much deeper than our emotional state, that is, it could be that there is no emotion, and this would say absolutely nothing about God being there or not in prayer. The spiritual state is much more profound than the emotional one. Our emotional state is only the superficial part. At times our faith sets us against our emotional make-up to free us from our possessiveness, from the identification we have made with it. Worse still when we have done so with our rational side, that is, with our thoughts. God must constantly destroy the castles we have built in our head, has to constantly set us against ourselves. It is the only way of convincing us we are free and that we don't need this. We can slip our moorings; we can make it and we need to battle to stay put like this woman, as obstinately as this woman. In this case too, I believe the gospel has brought us the example of a woman, to tell us that women are much more obstinate than men in the things that count, especially in the spiritual life. There are times in our life, I believe, when the Lord deliberately puts us to the test. Stupidly, Satan thinks he is winning. He doesn't know that in reality he is playing a part in sanctifying us. There is a whole plan behind tests of this kind. But there are times when we feel devoured: 'For the enemy has pursued me, crushing my life to the ground, making me sit in darkness like those long dead' (Ps 143:3). It is a struggle for liberation. It is the liberation of our true God.

All our Christian life, all our faith, is moving from being Simon to becoming Peter, following precisely the journey Simon Peter took. It is painful because we also have to go through betrayal, through the perception of our own limitations, the absence of God, of having understood nothing.

When we are emotionally humiliated in the spiritual life, and when we understand nothing, we pacify ourselves; we are in the maturity of spiritual life. I believe, from what I have understood from my little experience, that the last thing we will know at the end of our life is that we have understood almost nothing, and that is absolutely okay, because we are not our thoughts, not our feelings. Our ego is beneath all this. It is what Christ has liberated. He has not liberated us from our thoughts and feelings. We have feelings and we have thoughts but we are not our thoughts, not our feelings. The verb 'to have' and the verb 'to be' are important, because in the spiritual life, when these two dimensions are confused, it slips away from us. One can say: 'I am praying, but I have a negative feeling'; yes, you do, but you are not a negative feeling. You feel like you are a dog but you are not a dog. So be calm. Don't run. What holds us there? Faith: knowing that God loves me, not that He simply exists somewhere.

At a difficult moment of her spiritual life, St Teresa of Avila thought that at one stage of her struggle she had lost her faith. She was completely engulfed in the feeling of God's absence. She thought that she had mistaken her whole life, that nothing existed and she was fooled. But in the face of this, herewith her profession of faith: 'Even if the Lord, heaven and hell did not exist I would still love you because the love I have for you has no need of hope.'

Women often teach us the most beautiful words for making our true profession of faith.

2

Hope

(Or why what counts is almost always invisible)

Faith is not information about God, but information about the relationship between myself and God. If faith were simply information about God it could also be that it does not include me. Instead, it does concern me closely, because faith tells of a relationship between me and him. He has established this relationship. It is a relationship of love.

Whatever happens, I have an inherent certainty that he loves me. This is our strength, the faith which overcame the world, as the Word says.

So, if faith is the fact that God loves us, hope is believing that a hidden good underlies everything.

Faith concerns our relationship with God. Hope concerns our relationship with everything he created, including our life, ourselves. To hope means to live with the awareness that goodness is hidden in everything. There is always a good at the basis of everything.

When you have this awareness of underlying goodness, you need to live and make choices as a consequence. What could be a definition of hope in simple terms is provided for us by God's Word through two images: at a certain point the Word brings two mountains into a relationship: Tabor and Calvary.

Jesus takes his disciples, his friends, with him, disciples he had established a favourite connection with. Here, too, we need not be scandalised and indeed should note that God's love is not a uniform love but a preferential one — Jesus has his Peter, James and John. He has relationships he prefers. Preference, not equal choice, is the measure of love.

He took these three friends with him one day for a rather special trip in the countryside, up a mountain called Tabor. On this mountain, the Word tells us, 'he was transfigured' before their eyes. His clothes became dazzling white, such as no one on earth could bleach them, and Elijah and Moses appeared beside him (cf. Mk 9:2–8). Behind this image is the Christ who reveals his divinity. It is an experience of dazzling light which Jesus is giving his friends. He does so on purpose, as if he were suddenly opening up his humanity, his reality, and allowing his disciples to be able to glimpse what lies at the basis of everything, just for an instant. In that instant the disciples see the Son's divinity. They see it. The light is so powerful that they cannot keep their eyes open. The Gospel (Luke) tells us they were weighed down with sleep. I think Dante was very much inspired by the Gospel's description of their attitude when he writes in the *Divine Comedy*, for example: 'And then I fell as a dead body falls.' It is more or less like that in the Gospel before such beautiful experiences as those illuminations on Mt Tabor: the disciples are overcome by sleep, they swoon.

In Gethsemane, which is an experience of atrocious darkness, total depression, they are also weighed down by sleep. To sum it up, before the most important events in their life they sleep! This is not a rebuke, merely an observation. Our humanity is unable to keep its eyes open before great things like this, so we put in place all the strategies which we might call strategies of alienation. We need to distance ourselves to survive. We need to find means of escape. We all have our escape mechanisms, develop strategies to escape from what we are going through. This is something that at times we fail to understand, given the overly moralistic interpretations of contemporary societal analysis. Strategies like alcohol abuse, sexual misdemeanours, abuse of social media and the virtual world are not simply mistakes we make, but a form of dependence hiding this need for alienation and escape from things. We very often prefer to escape when we cannot manage life's drama, including when it is beautiful; we use alcohol, our affective side, our sexuality, social media, as an anaesthetic to put some distance between us and events.

The problem is not simply one of saying 'No, this is mistaken,' but of educating people to remain before grand moments, not be afraid to stand before them. It is the fear that overcomes a young person, for example, who falls in love and realises that this could be the person who accompanies him or her throughout life. When they hear 'throughout life' they run. And yet it is such a wonderful thing to find someone who fills our entire life. It should be so beautiful, yet it can weigh on us. Absolute choices weigh on us. As with illness, pain, we prefer to have laws that establish the right to die. What is euthanasia very often? The fact that we find pain, suffering, illness unbearable. We do not accept that at some point in our life we are no longer what we used to be, that our body degenerates. We are afraid of this and prefer euthanasia.

These general examples help to make us aware that at a personal, social and perhaps at a communal level too, we all develop flight strategies as the disciples did. But why is this Tabor experience interesting? Because Jesus knows well that the only way to manage the night is a burst of preventive light. He wants his disciples to be bathed in light. It is the only way to get them through the night. Tabor is necessary for Calvary. It is the experience of seeing, touching with our deepest selves the divinity of the Son of God which is at the basis of everything, this hidden good. When you know there is good hidden within, a day will come when everything is saying the opposite and only the memory of the light will save you. At the hour of the cross, the hour of Calvary, you no longer see the light, but only the memory of the light can stop you from running away. It is a profound memory reminding us that we once did see the light. This is what saves us in the night.

I believe that this memory of the light that saves us is very well described in the diary of a doctor who died of cancer. It is a memory based on simple but indelible things. In writing about the drama of illness, the fear, death, suffering at leaving his wife and children, he finds the indelible traces in himself of a memory of light, a Tabor that gives him strength. We should leave it to him to tell us directly:

> It will seem incredible, but what urges me at the moment to preserve hope binds me almost inexorably to a faith that the circumstances in themselves would not in the least justify. It is just an ordinary garden full of chamomile, a small plant bearing a myriad of tiny

flowers with a yellowy-gold corolla surrounded by a ring of small white petals. It is the memory of this encounter I had as a small child which has generated an unforgettable joy in me which now justifies my hope in Christ.

I was 5 years old and until then had lived in an apartment joined by a balcony to other apartments at Bovisa with my parents, two annoying sisters who mothered me, and our grandmother. Life at Bovisa was tough; I had to play on the floor of a narrow hallway with my only friend because games on the balcony bothered the neighbours. There was little to eat because of the war. I had to go to kindergarten every day where a very strict head teacher stood at the entrance checking all the children's scalps which moreover, were all shaven. Inside were the teachers for whom we had no respect or affection.

One evening, the sky over Bovisa was suddenly obscured by an incredible commotion of aeroplanes which we happily waved to from the balcony. When the first blasts came, our grandmother led us under the main entrance to the house. The explosions went on for an hour and one of them threw me into the air. I fell down on the floor unharmed. Since the bombardments were continuing, my parents decided to send us with our grandmother to Cerro where there was a house built by my grandfather Amedeo with the help of our friends and relatives before he died when still a very young man in France, where he worked as a seasonal brick layer.

I recall nothing of the trip to Cerro, but I do recall that as soon as I entered the large kitchen on the ground floor, and as if urged on by some mysterious force, I ran to open the door that looked out on the garden behind the house, and taking a couple of steps outside I seemed to be in paradise. I plunged almost up to my neck into a brilliant expanse, bathed in sunlight, of little yellow flowers with tiny white petals supported by a dark green covering of shrubs with almost thread-like leaves intertwined in a green tangle that hid any sign of earth.

I seemed to have lost all contact with the earth. The air was still. With my eyes overwhelmed by marvellous colours, my heart palpitating with joy, I cried, 'Grandma, come and see!' My grandmother, who was busy, looked out through the doorway and said, 'The garden is full of chamomile.'

It seems incredible, but the chamomile has forever conquered cancer and death in me. It is not true that someone dying of cancer goes through hell; it is not true that Rodolfo who died of a worse illness than cancer, went through hell. It is not true that death is the end of everything. It is not true because there was one brief instant in my life when there was a garden full of blooming chamomile, a feeling of joy and immense gratitude to the One who gave me life and that moment in life.

When we are faced with the 'revelation of truth,' when illness haunts us relentlessly in spasms of pain, we need to forget all the lectures we have given and heard, which once seemed to provide so much security, and now just make us angry. We need to fall silent and wait. It is life itself, going back to that memory again, which makes one see that in this 'truth' which now appears, there is much more than noting the inevitable pain and fragility of man. In this 'truth' in fact there is not only the present difficulty but also a memory.

> …This truth contains within it the irrefutable observation that the world is in the grip of evil, that our hope and our faith can do nothing against the evil that controls the world. Yet it also contains sudden flashes of light experienced and present in the memory, which testify to a merciful God inexorably hidden to our eyes, who awaits our recognition.
>
> From the moment I saw that garden, life became a marvellous adventure for me, full of a hope which, despite a thousand deviations and recoveries, has always been with me and impacted on my sometimes very poor, naive decisions in life: a hope that ultimately resists thinking that even now, the marvellous adventure has become unfortunately bestially painful and pitiless.

Each of us should have a Tabor which God has provided, a Tabor which we should absolutely connect with the Calvary we need to go through. This is what hope is! Hope is the living memory of this light that stays with us when darkness comes. It is having a field of chamomile which makes life worth living.

By contrast, Calvary is the experience of darkness. When faced with the cross, the disciples run away, because they do not see the Son of God but the failure of the Son of Man. They see the man of sorrows, a man disfigured, not transfigured. He is disfigured by pain, pierced by nails. There is nothing of beauty in this crucified man. Even the prophecies that refer to him say that the suffering servant was like one from whom others hide their faces: 'He was despised and rejected by others; a man of suffering acquainted with infirmity; and as one from whom others hide their faces he was despised, and we held him of no account' (Is 53:3).

They all run away, even his best friends. Only one remains, perhaps because he was unconscious: it is John, a mere teenager. Out of three, one remains beneath the cross. Even this should make us reflect. I believe the gospel recounts these flights so that none of us is afraid when the same thing occurs. Yet we saw him work miracles, we ate the loaves and fishes he multiplied, we saw him raise up Lazarus, the son of the widow of Nain, the daughter of Jairus. It does not matter, since at that moment it is as if all that memory were wiped out. We are overwhelmed by fear, terrified. We have an urge to run. Flight is the most human reaction we have for confronting life. We usually think of running before life's important things and the gospel recounts these flights to tell us, 'You are normal'. The saints are not people who never ran, but people who knew how to come back after running. Christ does not teach us the road where there is no escape, but a road to return by after we have done so. This is as wonderfully good as it is human. The darkness of the cross, of the death of the Son on the cross, is the experience of his humanity.

Immediate and mediated experience

Let us now compare Tabor and Calvary. What could we say about it all? That the experience of Calvary, that is, the experience of darkness, is always an immediate experience. The first thing we come up against is always what we see on Calvary. Instead, what we see on Tabor is mediated experience, not immediate, meaning it needs mediation. The light of Tabor is not immediate or visible.

The theological virtue of hope is not an immediate experience of good but a mediated one. Normally sickness, pain, suffering draw our immediate attention and have no need of other mediations, but good, yes it does; it needs mediation, meaning we have to dig down to find it. It is the treasure hidden in the field. To find a hidden treasure we need to dig. To find the precious pearl we need to open the oyster. Hope manifests in us as a kind of obstinacy which makes us dig into things until we find the good in them.

If we were locked up in a room full of light coming in through the windows, and were to close almost all the shutters, leaving just a glimmer of light, the first thing to happen would be to see nothing, at least until our eyes adjusted. When they begin to adjust, the dark is no longer dark and begins to become semi-darkness. You begin to see in the dark because your eyes are getting used to seeing the little bit of light coming through. The tiny bit of light filtering through the by-now-closed windows, helps us see the surroundings once more. Immediately, we cannot see in the dark, but if we can wait, at a certain point the darkness begins to reveal things. It is no longer pitch black, but a kind of light. Antonio Radari was right: ' We need to remain in the silence and wait.'

Hope is something of the kind, it is learning how to move in the dark, allowing the light in there somewhere to show some direction, just enough not to fall and not to have to stop.

It is very important that we convince ourselves of this: good exists, light exists, but they are not immediately visible to us. It takes patience, the patience to stay in the dark. What is it that gives us the strength to stay in the dark? The hope that the dark is not pitch black. What allows us to remain on the cross? The hope that the cross is not a cross through and through, meaning that a light is hidden there, a light underlying it all, a good.

If we take the Resurrection accounts, we see how true all this is. None of the appearances of the Risen Lord is immediate. No one immediately recognises Jesus, not even Mary Magdalene who runs into this man she mistakes for the gardener, or attendant (cf. Jn 20:1–18). No one immediately recognises him. They all need a mediation: a word – 'Mary!' 'Rabbuni!'; the empty tomb, a stranger who walks with you and reveals the meaning of the Scriptures, a nuisance on the shore who says, 'Haven't you caught any fish?' 'No!' 'Throw out your nets'; the mediation of those full nets; 'It is the Lord!' and Peter plunges into the water like an Olympian to get there (cf. Jn 21). The appearances of the Risen Lord tell us that the experience of encounter with the 'fact of the Resurrection' is always a mediated one.

I like to think that fundamentally, the Liturgy is this: the attempt to mediate the experience of the Risen Lord through gesture, smell, song, word. The good in this world, on Earth, in our life, is always an experience of mediation.

All this mediation has a theological foundation: it is the only way we can remain free. If good were immediate we would not be free – it would be evident to us and we would not have the option of choosing. Only in the half-light are we free, free when the light does not blind us. This is why Jesus becomes man, hides in the weakness of a baby, in the mediation of bread, wine, Eucharist. When the Eucharist is held up it does not blind us. We know the Lord is there, but it is the half-light of the Sacrament where we are also free to leave, pretend it is all not true, deny it. Freedom is being able to say that the empty tomb is proof he is not there, not proof that he is risen. We need to understand that all of our faith is based on an absence: everyone can read absence in a very human way. 'They stole the body; it was them.' For sure, it is most interesting that the soldiers are asleep: no one sees anything, yet it is much more reassuring to say: 'They have stolen the body' because the opposite would seem to be saying: 'He is risen!' (cf. Mt 28). It is this that distinguishes a believer from a non-believer: the Resurrection. But the Resurrection passes through the mediation of a sign that can also be misunderstood. It is not a clear sign: 'The tomb is empty. It is the clear sign of Christ's Resurrection.' No! The empty tomb is an ambiguous sign of what could be the Resurrection of Christ. Every now and again, throughout the Church's history, someone has rightly asked: why did the Lord not appear to everyone, confirming he was risen? We could also say that Jesus appeared many times over the forty days his disciples were hermits isolated in the Upper Room, but this experience of encountering him did not send them out. Fear had the better of them until Pentecost. It is the Spirit who dislodges them, not the simple experience of the Risen Lord. It is not said that because you see the Risen Lord, touch him, even put your finger in his wounds, eat the fish, the bread, this automatically makes you a better, more courageous person. The disciples were afraid and even when they see the Risen Lord are still afraid.

We say that it is Pentecost which hurls them out of the Upper Room, Pentecost of the Spirit, not simply experience. Not simply the Sacrament, the half-light, but the Spirit!

To describe this, Jesus gives us the example of the grain of wheat: 'Unless a grain of wheat falls into the earth and dies, it remains just a single grain; but if it does it bears much fruit.' (Jn 12:24). What does this mean? That if we take a seed and toss it into the soil, the immediate experience is to see the seed rot. But what is a synonym for rotting? That it begins to sprout. Hence, you see that something is coming apart in its form, but in reality another life is emerging. Rotting and sprouting are two sides of the same coin – you see it rotting but in reality it is sprouting. You see it dying but in reality it is living. You see it losing but in reality it is winning. Through this example Christ is telling us that what we see with our eyes, Calvary, is only the reverse side of Tabor. The man defeated on the Cross is simply the reverse side of the man who has conquered death and is no longer the same life as before, but a different life. The Resurrection is not a new seed: the Resurrection is the shoot. We will not be given back to the same life. This life of ours is a seed. Paul says: 'Just as we have borne the image of the man of dust, we will also bear the image of the man of heaven' (cf. 1 Cor 15:35–38); here we are only potentially something; there we will see Him as He is.

The Resurrection is something radically different. But it begins, in that instant, from what exists now. What does all this mean? That the Cross I am experiencing, the Calvary, the darkness I am submerged in is only a part of the larger picture. The Resurrection always begins by sprouting, that is, with the experience of rotting, of something coming apart. Dying to ourselves means sprouting, not simply diminishing.

We could imagine a farmer going up to a seed and saying: 'I made a mistake taking you from the sack and throwing you into the soil, because now you are beginning to rot. I don't like seeing you rot so I'll take you out of the soil and put you back in the sack.' That is death! We are taken from the logic in which suffering is enlightened by a basic light. It is the light of the shoot glimpsed in the seed by a gift of God. None of us has eyes strong enough to be able to see the shoot hidden within the seed. The theological virtue of hope is having the inner certainty, the inner glance which intuits the shoot within the seed, the victory within the failure. 'Lord, I am losing everything, I am dying. I have nothing more, but I have hope,' is the intuition that within all the pain, the failure, something is hidden, a good, the shoot. We do not know how to say it, how to describe it, because hope is believing that a good exists even though we cannot describe it. It should sound like this: 'I do not know the meaning of my life, but I know that such exists.' It is faith in the existence of a meaning even when we do not ultimately understand it.

The reference figure who can accompany us in understanding this is someone who, were we to interpret him without faith as a key, we would consider to be a figure of dire misfortune. This is Joseph in the Old Testament, the man sold by his brothers. We will use him as a witness, not as a good example, because good examples are ideal models which have us say: 'I will never be like that.' Instead witnesses are those who manage within their own limitations and what they properly desire. Joseph is such a witness, someone who always finds a way to stay on his feet amid so many problems. He is truly a man of hope, so let us understand some of the encouragement we receive from his life and gifts.

Joseph of Egypt's Cross

We have climbed two mountains in the gospel, Tabor and Calvary. We have understood how hope can be a mediated experience of light. It is the inner certainty that behind the darkness which is our immediate experience, a light is hidden. Knowing how to remain in the dark means allowing the light to gradually create a semi-darkness needed to be able to pass through the darkness.

Darkness is not only darkness. Whoever lives in hope knows it is not so dark.

But before beginning to touch on something of the experience of our witness, Joseph of Egypt sold by his brothers, I would like to spend a moment with the mystery of the cross.

I would like to offer a definition of the cross which I hope can serve as a spiritual reinterpretation of our own experience.

What is the cross? The cross is real in as much as it is what I have before me.

We are led to believe that the cross is an event in life, a particular circumstance, or in some cases, person. But the cross always concerns reality in its totality. It is the reality surrounding us which we do not always choose. We certainly do choose part of that reality, but the vast majority of things in that reality are not of our own choosing yet there they are. They exist. Jesus says that whoever wants to follow him must deny him or herself and take up their cross daily (cf. Mt 16:24). Translated this means that those who wish to be his disciples must take on the burden of reality there before them in all its totality.

If we were to reason in familiar terms we would reason thus, without irony and with great openness of heart: 'The cross is my husband, just as he is; my wife, just the way she is; my children, the way they are.' Or, the cross can be the fact of not succeeding in having children, work, colleagues, neighbours, in-laws, friends, even our own story. Much of the reality around us we acknowledge as not being fundamentally of our own choosing; there is part of our reality that escapes our calculation, our freedom, yet it exists, it is before us.

Taking up our own cross means feeling responsible for all the reality before us and not only the bit we like. We are responsible also for the bit that is not our choice. Christ asks us to love him by loving everything real, not only the bit that interests us or which is convenient. It is too simplistic to love the Lord only with what pleases us. The problem is learning to love him also with what does not please us. In this sense the cross sanctifies us because at some point we understand that what lies before us is precisely the opportunity the Lord is giving us to love Him.

Given this preamble, let us enter into the story of Joseph, bearing in mind what is written in Leviticus: 'You should not hate in your heart any of your kin' (Lev 19:17).

Joseph's experience is the complete opposite of this command in Leviticus. He is one of the most famous victims of brotherly hatred.

The contents of the Book of Genesis are bracketed by failed brotherly relationships: at the beginning of Genesis is the story of two brothers, Cain and Abel, and at the end, the story of Joseph and his brothers. Very interesting this, as if the Word were suggesting to us that the decisive place where we experience our failures, our humanness, our life, is always in brotherly or sisterly relationships. Yet we should make a distinction between siblings and friends. We can choose our friends, relationships of choice, but we cannot choose our brothers and sisters. They are a given.

Sibling relationships are a given, beyond our choice. They just are. Inevitably in our communities and families, which are a gift, there are always the less than beautiful ingredients of our humanity: jealousy, envy, at times violence, death, homicide (there are many ways to kill Abel). Very often all the jealousy comes from the fact that the father loves one in a special, unrepeatable way. It often happens that when we compare our relationship with others we think the others are the favourites, even in spiritual terms. We all suffer a bit from the 'Joseph syndrome.' It is a spiritual, psychological and emotional sickness which manifests as profound bitterness, telling us that our brother/sister is loved more than us. The Joseph syndrome means being the target of others because they think you are more loved than they are.

But we see where the problem is with Joseph, He is the son of an old man and his father Jacob has a tender eye for this son of his, the firstborn of his wife Rachel.

It will do us well to directly read the beginning of his story:

> Joseph, being seventeen years old, was shepherding the flock with his brothers; he was a helper to the sons of Bilhar and Zilpah, his father's wives; and Joseph brought a bad report of them to their father. Now Israel loved Joseph more than any other of his children, because he was the son of his old age; and he had made him a long robe with sleeves. But when his brothers saw that their father loved him more than

> all his brothers, they hated him, and could not speak peaceably to him.
>
> Once Joseph had a dream, and when he told it to his brothers, they hated him even more. He said to them, 'Listen to this dream that I dreamed. There we were, binding sheaves in the field, suddenly my sheaf rose and stood upright; then your sheaves gathered around it and bowed down to my sheaf.' His brothers said to him, 'Are you indeed to reign over us? Are you indeed to have dominion over us?' So they hated him even more because of his dreams and his words.
>
> He had another dream and told it to his brothers saying, 'Look, I have had another dream: the sun, the moon and eleven stars were bowing down to me,' But when he told it to his father and to his brothers, his father rebuked him and said, 'What kind of dream is this that you have had? Shall we indeed come, I and your mother and brothers, and bow to the ground before you?' So his brothers were jealous of him but his father kept the matter in mind (Gen 37:2–11).

Predilection, which should be such a very beautiful thing, in reality manifests as a complication in our lives. When you are especially loved like that you become very complex, just as happened to Joseph. He was his father's beloved (love is always predilection) and this creates an endless number of problems for him with his brothers. Symbolically it all revolves around a cloak, a gift to Joseph from his father. It comes to mind that perhaps the proof that God is in our lives is exactly the degree to which it is complicated.

However, there is another ingredient which complicates the scene: Joseph has a gift of dreaming and interpreting dreams. In the East this ability is very much linked to God, a kind of revelation, knowing how to read events from within. St Ignatius would call this 'the gift of discernment.' Well, Joseph has the gift of discernment. This should make his life simpler, should be an advantage. But no, it becomes a further motive for envy. Another complication. The talents the Lord gives us do not make our lives simpler but complicate it. When we are blinded by the 'Joseph syndrome' we even look on talents given by the Lord in a bad light.

At times, the talents the Lord gives us are also the cause of a heap of evils we experience in our lives. They can become a curse or our salvation. What decides this? Our freedom.

But let's take a step back. The passage from Genesis says, 'they hated him and could not speak peaceably to him.' They have a communication problem. When there is a communication problem, inevitably its consequences have an impact on communion. Communion and communication share the same root. When one no longer communicates one is no longer in communion with. When there is a crisis of communication, a crisis of the word, there is also a crisis of communion between people. Where does this closure lead?

> Now his brothers went to pasture their father's flock near Shechem. And Israel said to Joseph, 'Are not your brothers pasturing the flock at Shechem? Come, I will send you to them.' He answered, 'Here I am.' So he said to him, 'Go now, see if it is well with your brothers and with the flock; and bring word back to me.' So he sent him from the valley of Hebron.
>
> He came to Shechem, and a man found him wandering in the fields; the man asked him 'What are

you seeking?' 'I am seeking my brothers,' he said; 'tell me please, where they are pasturing the flock.' The man said, 'They have gone away, for I heard them say, 'Let us go to Dothan.'' So Joseph went after his brothers and found them at Dothan. They saw him from a distance, and before he came near to them, they conspired to kill him. They said to one another, 'Here comes this dreamer. Come now, let us kill him and throw him into one of the pits; then we shall say that a wild animal has devoured him and we shall see what will become of his dreams.' But when Reuben heard it, he delivered him out of their hands saying, 'Let us not take his life.' Reuben said to them, 'Shed no blood; throw him into this pit here in the wilderness but lay no hands on him' – that he might rescue him out of their hand and restore him to his father. So when Joseph came to his brothers, they stripped him of his robe, the long robe with sleeves that he wore; and they took him and threw him into a pit. The pit was empty; there was no water in it.

Then they sat down to eat; and looking up they saw a caravan of Ishmaelites coming from Gilead, with their camels carrying gum, balm, and resin, on their way to carry it down to Egypt. Then Judah said tho his brothers, 'What profit is it if we kill our brother and conceal his blood? Come, let us sell him to the Ishmaelites, and not lay our hands on him, for he is our brother, our own flesh.' And his brothers agreed. When some Midianite traders passed by, they drew Joseph up, lifting him out of the pit, and sold him to the Ishmaelites for twenty pieces of silver. And they took Joseph to Egypt.

When Reuben returned to the pit and saw that Joseph was not in the pit, he tore his clothes. He returned to

> his brothers and said, 'The boy is gone and I, where can I turn?' Then they took Joseph's robe, slaughtered a goat, and dipped the robe in the blood. They had the long robe with sleeves taken to their father, and they said, 'This we have found; see now whether it is your son's robe or not.' He recognised it and said, 'It is my son's robe! A wild animal has devoured him; Joseph is without doubt torn to pieces.' Then Jacob tore his garments, and put sackcloth on his loins, and mourned for his son many days. All his sons and all his daughters sought to comfort him; but he refused to be comforted, and said, 'No, I shall go down to Sheol to my son, mourning.' Thus his father bewailed him. Meanwhile the Midianites had sold him in Egypt to Potiphar one of Pharaoh's officials, the Captain of the guard. (Gen 37:12–36).

A number of years went by as a slave. Years, not days. Within this slavery his human qualities, which were of the highest degree, his great tenderness and righteousness, won him the favour of Potiphar. Potiphar began to trust him with responsibility in his house, and Joseph repaid this trust by transforming Potiphar's house, gardens, goods.

> Now Joseph was taken down to Egypt and Potiphar, an officer of Pharaoh, the Captain of the guard, an Egyptian, bought him from the Ishmaelites who had brought him down there. The Lord was with Joseph, and he became a successful man; he was in the house of his Egyptian master. His master saw that the Lord was with him, and that the Lord caused all that he did to prosper in his hands. So Joseph found favour in his sight and attended him; he made him overseer of his house and put him in charge of all that he had. From

> the time that he made him overseer in his house and over all that he had, the Lord blessed the Egyptian's house for Joseph's sake; the blessing of the Lord was on all that he had, in house and field. So he left all that he had in Joseph's charge; and, with him there, he had no concern for anything but the food that he ate (Gen 39:2–6).

Joseph begins to go up in the world. It seems that life is finally showing him good favour, until Potiphar's wife takes a fancy to him.

> Now Joseph was handsome and good-looking. And after a time his master's wife cast her eyes on Joseph and said, 'Lie with me.' But he refused and said to his master's wife, 'Look, with me here, my master has no concern about anything in the house, and he has put everything that he has in my hand. He is not greater in this house than I am, nor has he kept back anything from me except yourself, because you are his wife. How then could I do this great wickedness, and sin against God?' And although she spoke to Joseph day after day, he would not consent to lie beside her or to be with her. One day, however, when he went into the house to do his work, and while no one else was in the house, she caught hold of his garment, saying, 'Lie with me!' But he left his garment in her hand, and fled and ran outside. When she saw that he had left his garment in her hand and had fled outside, she called out to the members of her household and said to them, 'See, my husband has brought among us a Hebrew to insult us! He came in to lie with me, and I cried out with a loud voice: and when he heard me raise my voice and cry out, he left his garment beside

> me, and fled outside.' Then she kept his garment by her until his master came home, and she told him the same story, saying, 'The Hebrew servant, whom you have brought among us, came into me to insult me; but as soon as I raised my voice and cried out, he left his garment beside me and fled outside.'
>
> When his master heard the words that his wife spoke to him saying, 'This is the way your servant treated me,' he became enraged. And Joseph's master took him and put him into the prison, the place where the king's prisoners were confined; he remained there in prison (Gen 39:6–20).

Reading the story of Joseph, what comes to mind is that good is always a precarious gift which one can lose from one moment to the next. All the adventures, injustices and vicissitudes this young man has to endure make us ask: Why? Why all this pain? Why does God not intervene? Why does he not defend a righteous man?

But the story of Joseph continues. He is even well liked in the king's prison:

> But the Lord was with Joseph and showed him steadfast love; he gave him favour in the sight of the chief jailer. The chief jailer committed to Joseph's care all the prisoners who were in the prison, and whatever was done there, he was the one who did it. The chief jailer paid no heed to anything that was in Joseph's care, because the Lord was with him; and whatever he did the Lord made it prosper (Gen 39:21–23).

There are still years of prison, until Pharaoh's nightmares remind him of Joseph's ability to interpret dreams. Once again, Joseph emerges from the depths of the netherworld which is the prison and gradually becomes the most important person in Egypt after Pharaoh. But this is not the most decisive thing about his life. Before coming to the point, we should have the courage to ask ourselves: What do we do to preserve hope when the one who loves you like your father thinks you are dead? When your only hope is being locked up in prison, what do you do? Yet Joseph is a masterpiece of hope. This man makes the effort to remain in the dark until he is once again reached by the light.

It is especially at a time of general darkness, a famine this time that covers the whole land, that his brothers are forced to go to Egypt to beg for bread. They do not know that the man handing out the victuals is their brother. They do not recognise him. He recognises them but holds back from human and understandable revenge. After putting them to the test he finally plucks up the courage to reveal himself and offer them, and us, a beautiful interpretation of his story. The scene recounted in Genesis is extraordinary and beautiful. Joseph asked his brothers, unaware of his identity, to bring their youngest brother, Benjamin, to Egypt. They do so but by way of a subterfuge, Joseph puts a silver cup in Benjamin's sack. Asking for a search at the last moment he has the sacks emptied and it looks like Benjamin is guilty. The verdict is for Benjamin to be retained as a slave. The brothers who had once sold Joseph now act differently. They try to save their brother from his fate. Judah even offers to take his youngest brother's place.

Faced with all this, Joseph can no longer hold back:

> Then Joseph could no longer control himself before all those who stood by him, and he cried out, 'Send

everyone away from me.' So no one stayed with him when Joseph made himself known to his brothers. And he wept so loudly that the Egyptians heard it, and the house of Pharaoh heard it. Joseph said to his brothers, 'I am Joseph. Is my father still alive?' But his brothers could not answer him, so dismayed were they at his presence.

Then Joseph said to his brothers, 'Come closer to me' And they came closer. He said, 'I am your brother, Joseph, whom you sold into Egypt. And now do not be distressed, or angry with yourselves, because you sold me here; for God sent me before you to preserve life. For the famine has been in the land these two years: and there are five more years in which there will be neither ploughing nor harvest. God sent me before you to preserve for you a remnant on earth, and to keep alive for you many survivors. So it was not you who sent me here, but God; he has made me a father to Pharaoh, and lord of all his house and ruler over all the land of Egypt. Hurry and go up to my father and say to him, 'Thus says your son Joseph, God has made me lord of all Egypt; come down to me, do not delay. You shall settle in the land of Goshen, and you shall be near me, you and your children, and your children's children, as well as your flocks, your herds, and all that you have. I will provide for you there-since there are five more years of famine to come-so that you and your household, and all that you have, will not come to poverty.' And now your eyes and the eyes of my brother Benjamin see that it is my own mouth that speaks to you. You must tell my father how greatly I am honoured in Egypt and all that you have seen. Hurry and bring my father down here.' Then he fell upon his brother Benjamin's neck and wept, while Benjamin

> wept upon his neck. And he kissed all his brothers and wept upon them; and after that his brothers talked with him (Gen 45:1–15).

What strikes us most is the wise interpretation Joseph offers of his story: 'I endured all this pain, all this hell, because God meant to love all of us through my suffering. It is not you who brought me here but God who led me here.'

What is Joseph's immediate experience? To feel that he is the victim of his brother's injustice. What is the wise interpretation of his life, mediated through hope? That God led him there. God allowed all this because he had a much larger plan in mind through his suffering. What does Joseph's suffering teach? That at times with patience we must take up our cross, the cross before us especially when we do not understand it. Like Joseph we need to reason thus 'If this reality exists, this cross that lies before me, then God has a plan for it, for this suffering. God is pointing to a good which is not simply a good for me but a good for everyone, starting with me. If I step back from this cross, this darkness, not only will I deprive myself of this light, but I will deprive a whole people.'

The fate of an entire people depends on my patience before the cross, my staying in the dark, in hope.

God is greater than the evil and injustice of these brothers. He is greater and so great that it is futile wasting time and saying: 'How terrible evil is.' It is better to say, 'How great good is,' which also contains my brother's perfidy and mediocrity. When you live like this you know you are truly working for what is good.

Fundamentally, this is hope: it is knowing how to stay with things before the cross, not because we see a solution but because we have the sure confidence that God is carrying out his work. If we were not, this reality would not be happening. If it is, even if it hurts us and weighs on us, God is weaving a story of salvation. This is what my 'Here I am' requires of me.

It converts us and reconciles us with our story, has us embrace Benjamin and burst into tears. And especially, it reopens communion because the communication links have been restored: 'Then he fell upon his brother Benjamin's neck and wept, while Benjamin wept upon his neck. And he kissed all his brothers and wept upon them; and after that his brothers talked with him.'

Most of our suffering comes from the fact that we do not accept reality as it lies before us. We feel bad because reality does not correspond to our expectations. Instead, it is precisely here that the opportunity lies for our holiness. It is because it does not correspond to our expectations that we can learn to love. Jesus translates this idea in Matthew's Gospel as follows: 'For if you love those who love you, what reward do you have? Do not even the tax collectors do the same?' (Mt 5:46). That is, if you love those who it is convenient to love, are not all who do likewise good? But loving when it is not convenient – this is what makes saints of us. It is learning, like Mary, to remain beneath the cross, even when it is terrible looking at one's son dying beneath one's eyes. Well then, we can do no other than link the virtue of hope, the theological virtue of hope, to a human attitude which is patience: 'Love is patient' St Paul says (1 Cor 13:4). In Christian art there is one icon of Christ known as *Christus patiens*. It is of Jesus bound, crowned with thorns, flogged and suffering, but in a pose of extreme meekness, almost as if he wishes to bear all that suffering with infinite patience. It seems like an heroic attitude, but it is not heroic. It is shrewd. If you do not know how to swim and fall into the water and thrash about, you immediately go under, but if you stay calm you float. Patience produces this within us. When we thrash about beneath the cross we are crushed, go under. When we learn patience, through grace, it is a law of gravity of God's grace that we stay afloat, we do not drown, we live. It is the unimaginable fullness of life that comes from the cross, comes from patience with the cross.

I believe we can each look at our own story and see that there is a beloved Joseph within us which has created a whole heap of problems. But the logic of Joseph's brothers is also part of us. We are constantly the favourites but also at odds with others.

Within, is always the logic of predilection and thus of the flesh: envy, jealousy, anger etc.; St Paul names all these attitudes with some precision (cf. Gal 5:18–21).

The old and the new man in us struggle between them. However it is an unequal struggle because the Lord has given more to the spiritual man. This 'more' is the theological virtues. He has given the spiritual man hope, and this conquers absolutely, says Paul: 'No, in all these things we are more than conquerors through him who loved us' (Rom 8:37).

This awareness, when it reaches the heart, changes everything. At that moment we understand that we no longer need to ask God for a different life – it is a different heart we need to ask God for, a heart that recognises and knows how to treasure Christ's love: the treasure of light hidden beneath every darkness.

3

Charity

(Or why love comes first, the rest pales)

We need to have the courage to say that what lies at the basis of our life is not faith in the first place. If there is one foundational virtue in our life, this is charity.

Every human life is perceived to be human only if we see that love is the ground on which it is based. When we do not perceive this prime basis, this preventive good, everything seems unbearable.

Faith is believing that God loves me.

Hope is knowing that there is a good underpinning everything that exists.

So, to provide a definition of charity we should say this: charity is knowing that before all else, before everything, there is love.

The difference between this and hope is subtle but decisive. If hope tells us there is a good underlying everything, charity tells us that the first good of all is an underlying foundational love.

This completely changes the definition of Christianity, because rightly so, we have always been taught that

Christianity is to love, yet this is the consequence of Christianity, because in its prime nature it is something else.

Christianity is knowing we are loved. Being Christian does not mean only living by the commandment to love. Yes, the commandment is to love but also to allow ourselves to be loved. This is the mainstay of our life. This is the requirement for life to remain human because the heart of the human being, believer or non-believer, Christian or non-Christian, demands by nature to know that it is loved.

We become ill when we do not feel this. Everyone looks for love. We all seek to be loved. Most of our pathologies come from love, that is, not feeling loved in a radical and decisive way. These pathologies take on a variety of appearances, modes, a whole range of disturbances, but by far the greater number of human problems spring from this root of love not met or not given. When there is no fundamental correspondence within us to this great desire, this huge desire for love, we begin to feel ill. What is more disturbing is that not even having faith secures us from the need for love, charity. It is not just me saying this but Paul: 'If I have all faith so as to move mountains, but do not have love, I am nothing' (cf. 1 Cor 13:2).

There could also be a community, family, a human consensus very much faith-filled but we do not say that it thereby automatically has the experience of love, of charity. This is why we sometimes feel bad despite the evidence of faith, because the only thing that satisfies our heart even more than faith, more than hope, is love, knowing we are loved in a stable, clean-cut and decisive manner. When we do not feel this radical sense of being loved, we can also have faith but we are not safe from feeling bad in human terms. On the contrary, it sets up a kind of anxiety in us, a split, a struggle: 'I have faith but I feel bad. How come? I believe God exists but I feel bad. How is that possible? I see there is good underpinning my life but I continue to feel depressed. How is that? I am a practising Catholic, have a regular sacramental life, am in God's grace, yet I continue to be weighed down by anxiety. How can that be?'

Only love cures our anxiety, our sadness, discomfort, lack of satisfaction. Only love! God sends his Son into the world to take seriously this desire we all have to feel loved.

God knows all too well that we cannot be satisfied with commandments. Commandments do not make us feel loved. It is not precepts, not the Word itself that makes us feel loved; not the simple information that comes from heaven telling us, 'You are loved.' It is not information that changes our life. Love, like true faith, is either experienced or it is not, in which case it is useless. Charity which becomes mere information does not help. This is why God no longer gives us commandments and precepts. He gives us his Son. He knows we need the concreteness of love, not just the explanation of love. We do not only need it to be explained how we go about loving but first of all need to 'know we are loved, ' to 'feel loved.'

Our spiritual life, our Christian life, consists of something very simple: in allowing God to love us. This, by way of summary, is the aim of the spiritual life.

But this is also one of the most difficult things, because we have become masters at placing obstacles before such an experience. We immediately set up a moral perspective in ourselves, where it is we who have to do the loving and we move on to the consequences of charity, cutting out the motivation for why we need to love. By reinterpreting our spiritual life, our sacramental life and life of faith from this perspective of 'letting myself be loved,' we upend our whole way of seeing things. Why should I go to Mass? To let myself be loved, not first of all because 'I must', like a commandment external to me, forcing me. Why do I read the gospel? To let myself be loved. Why receive the Eucharist? To let myself be loved. Why choose a vocation? To let myself be loved in that specific vocation. If there is one thing that motivates our life, it is in knowing that every gesture in life and in our spiritual life is to allow him to love us even before we love him, and others as a response to that. When we lose sight of this it all becomes dramatic: loving becomes dramatic. It becomes frustrating for us to have to love our brothers and sisters, to have to love God, because we feel like cracked cisterns as the Prophet says, containing nothing, dry, and at the same time everyone is coming to draw from us. We have nothing, but people keep taking, and at times we feel we are going crazy, because people keep asking. Our brothers and sisters, our family, our friends, the community, even God keeps asking. But I have nothing! What can I give? 'If I speak in the tongues of mortals and of angels' says Paul, which translated means that even if I were very intelligent and had all the libraries of the world in my head, 'but do not have love, I am nothing' (cf. 1 Cor 13:1–2). Knowing everything without feeling loved is no help to me at all.

We can even constantly fall into that subtle form of heresy, perversion of faith called Gnosticism, by thinking that problems are resolved by forever learning more, reading, reasoning, living in a purely cerebral way. We ask, consult, keep adding to what we know but despite it all we feel empty, dissatisfied, because it is not 'knowing' that changes our life. Love is what fills our life. Our knowledge is no help to us without love.

'If I give away all my possessions, and if I hand over my body so that I may boast, but do not have love, I gain nothing' (1 Cor 13:3). If I were to sacrifice myself, die a martyr, even give my life for my brother, but did not have love, it would be no help at all. I can even give my life and not have love. What does that mean? That someone who has given their life has not done it out of love? It is something much more serious: we can give our life because we think it is right to do so, but not because we felt loved to the extent of giving our life. The gesture is the same but what it produces in us is different.

Everything we do in life either comes from the fact that we feel loved, or it inevitably becomes a duty which then becomes frustration or a feeling of guilt. It is frustration when we do our duty but do not feel happy despite it. Instead, it is a feeling of guilt when we do not even manage to do our duty because we do not find the strength.

Hence, we should be saying that charity is the prerequisite for life.

Descartes tells us: '*Cogito ergo sum*,' 'I think, therefore I am.' We should say likewise: 'I am loved, therefore I am.'

Even in my little experience, I have gone through stages where I thought, for example, that a certain kind of penitential life would have helped me and brought spiritual growth as well. Over time, however, I became aware that this penitential life, these choices, the small or the bigger renunciations I sought to make, were only superstructures. I realised that Christ never asked me to fast as a superstructure but only when I conceive of fasting as a consequence of my 'being loved': I feel so loved that I can also share in his sufferings. I can also do something – 'In my flesh I am completing what is lacking in Christ's affliction,' as Paul says (Col 1:24). We could almost say: 'Paul, you are a heretic! Christ saved us completely.' 'Certainly,' Paul would reply 'but not like you think.' The 'In my flesh I am completing what is lacking' is something extraordinary that Christ allows us to do. He deliberately leaves a small empty space to be filled by us, but for it to be filled by us with the same love that urged him on. It is a love not completed out of duty, necessity, rule, penance, as an end in itself, but completed because we have begun to live and feel alive as Christ lived and felt alive. What is it that makes Christ Christ? His knowing that he was loved by the Father. At his baptism Jesus heard the voice say, 'Here is my beloved;' it is there we discover Jesus' secret. Jesus is not living a life in mistaken obedience to his Father – his is not a life which simply executes what the Father wants. His obedience is born of love, that is, from feeling loved by the Father. Love precedes Christ's mission on this earth. It is the Father's love which establishes the Son. We should ask: what is charity? Charity is the love the Father has for the Son. This is charity! When we ask for the gift of charity we are asking for the same love the Father has for the Son, not something akin to it but the same.

There is an alternative way of naming the love the Father has for the Son: the Holy Spirit. Either we reinterpret everything, knowing that the Lord wants to reach us through love, or everything is empty, sterile, grey, brings us no fullness, no happiness. When there is a need to renew ourselves personally and as a community, I believe that the departure point is firstly that every single rule, rite and decision, all the gestures for example of a community, family, a relationship, must always begin with this assumption: 'Does what we do and how we do it make us feel loved?' Yes? Then it is all going well – No? Then there are some problems we have to solve.

There is no need, at times, to distort things, because what counts is not defending something to the bitter end, even when it is empty. We must defend to the ultimate, God's will that we feel loved, and we should measure things out to this end. Renewal is never about turning something inside out. Renewal functions in the same way as tuning an instrument. You don't need to change the instrument, just adjust the strings in such a way that they come back into harmony. We always need the ability to tune everything in our personal and community life, the tuning fork being God's will that we feel loved. Do you feel loved? This is the aim of the tuning. It is from there we need to begin; our families, relationships, communities, are either based on love or they don't exist.

Either my life is based on charity or we do not have a life!

The departure point is to let God do this, because in the desire to be loved three things are hidden: belonging, meaning and destination.

Belonging

Love makes us feel that we belong to someone.

More often than not, we experience the insecurity of constantly feeling we lack something, that we are orphans, vagrants. Charity makes us pilgrims, not just vagrants, because God gives us belonging: 'You are mine.'

Little children teach us better than others how we should live our spiritual life. I understood this watching them play at the seaside so often. The ones who seem most lively and carefree are very often this way because they feel safe in the presence of their mother and father. Under their gaze they have the freedom to amuse themselves and even go beyond the normal limits. They go into deep water because they know someone is watching out for them, ready to intervene. Obviously they don't think all this through, but unconsciously feel sure enough to be daring. Children who are overly cautious, quiet, calm, perhaps never go far from the bank or shore, and always play inside the same square metre, almost seem to be demonstrating a kind of insecurity in their apparent calm. They do not feel safe and so stay put in a well-defined area.

I could almost say that the proof children feel loved or not lies in the degree to which they are carefree. It is the fact that they feel safe which drives them to test the limits. It is not about rules, but I believe this example renders the idea of what love does when it gives us a sense of belonging. We can only enter deep water when we know there is someone on the shore, if we have a sense of belonging in our life that inwardly authorises us to dare, go beyond.

It is in this sense that we can also say: 'Lord, what do you radically want of me? What is my deep water? What are the bounds I need to go beyond?'

A relationship, too, can be contained within limits, living within a discipline, but it is the sense of belonging which, at times, brings us back to the Spirit who tells us to go beyond, set out into the deep, not be satisfied, dare to say: 'It is not enough for me to remain just in the present moment. I want to love you forever, for my entire life.' Deep water is loving someone forever, making ultimate choices, daring big things. It is the Spirit who does this because love has given us a sense of belonging, a certainty which enables us.

A child's sleep or insomnia is also revealing of this dynamic. Normally a small child has disturbed sleep patterns when it does not feel safe in its relationships. Each of us, but babies especially, lowers our defences and sleeps when we feel secure. If children do not feel secure, they never lower defences, always keep an eye open, suffer from insomnia, the inability to consign themselves to the unknown land of sleep where they are completely defenceless. We can rest, only when we feel safe. In the spiritual life or in Christian life, things work the same way. What allows us to rest in the Spirit, in the ability to remain in the Lord, comes from the fact that we feel we belong.

We can only taste and enjoy life when we feel we belong to someone, otherwise we feel something is wrong, and it shows up as one or other form of insecurity, the symptoms of which can also be excessive attachment to ideas, rules, structures which in real terms do not speak of fidelity but fear.

Meaning

The second characteristic is meaning.

Love fills life with meaning.

We could sum up the first symptom that love is lacking as follows: what we experience has no taste, seems futile, seems to be without meaning. All this can be fearful. But when someone feels there is no meaning, they should not just stare at the emptiness but see that the problem is more radical, that the serious problem lies in love. The emptiness is often bound up with the lack of feeling loved. Some studies tell us there is an exponential increase in youthful depression and eating disorders. Many young people suffering these things are helped by simply tackling the management of the symptom. For example, the attempt to cure anorexia by trying to re-educate the individual to eat, relate to food. But this is not where the root problem lies. Most of these symptoms stem from the fact that these young people do not feel well-liked, do not feel loved, and so express their discomfort this way, and load up their bodies with the problem. The fault lies with relationships, not with the mechanics of the body.

So many of the pathologies in our societies, even in our communities, are not solved simply by taking the problem as it expresses itself. Very often it stems from the fact that we do not feel well-liked. This can result in division, conflict, but no division, no conflict is resolved merely by establishing arrangements for peace. In truth, we are at war, but have established a peace agreement to cover the rest of the conflict between us. One could say: 'Our community is united' even when it is not true. We have settled our divisions with peace settlements that are a fiction, artificial ways of hiding the true nature of the tension. We can settle division only by going to the root, because if we feel loved, many of the tings that divide us disappear. If we do not feel loved, even a teaspoon falling to the floor is good reason to get stirred up!

Destination

The third characteristic is destination.

Love gives us a destiny.

However, I would immediately like to free our imagination from the idea that destiny means that what we have to do is written down somewhere.

Destiny is a destination. What is the destination of each of us? To return home to him. How we return is up to us. Mysteriously, God gives us grace to accompany us, but normally it is our freedom which decides the way we return. The worst thing that can happen to a person is not to have a home to return to, not to feel he or she has a destiny.

Here is the other thing that strikes us profoundly: waking up in the morning and not having a valid reason to make the day ahead worth living, a valid destiny, one that responds to the question: where am I heading? It moves me so much to know that the Lord gives us belonging and a destiny, a departure and arrival point. This makes the journey possible. This makes life possible.

Knowing we are loved is to know we have a home we are heading for, to have a reason for waking up, to know that everything we do has a direction.

What is the work of evil in all this? If God wants to make us feel loved, then evil is precisely the opposite; it gives us all the reasons why we should not feel we are loved.

What is sin? In the first instance it is not transgression. Sin is an obstacle to feeling we are loved. In this sense it leads us to death. It is not simply breaking a rule that leads us to death, but the fact that sin separates us from love. This is what destroys us. The vast majority of our sins are our attempts to feel loved, to be happy, since one cannot love oneself in isolation. For love to be effective we need to receive it.

Sometimes we behave like people who have fallen down a well and try to pull themselves out by the hair. It is an illusion we very often fall into, especially in the spiritual life. Instead, love is always the intervention of someone outside the well, lowering themselves into the well to pull us out. This gesture of lowering oneself to the bottom of the well is what theology calls *kenosis*. This *kenosis,* the descent, is the Son; God coming down the well in our history to rescue us. What should we do? Let him do it! Spiritual life is the attempt to hinder, as little as possible, the work of salvation God carried out through his Son, who comes to rescue us from the depths of non-meaning. It is allowing love to save us by coming down into the depths of ourselves. If you water a plant with a strong jet of water, the water pours over it but does not get right into it. Usually drip-feed efforts are more effective because the slowness of the water falling enables it to penetrate deeper. In appearance the approach seems slower, less effective, but it is precisely the opposite. Spiritual life functions like a drip-feed. Spiritual life with too much force is like a running hose that does not penetrate. What penetrates at depth is the slowness of water working its way down.

Our real problem is the separation we have created between head and heart. We know lots of things but the problem is getting them to reach the heart, allowing love to result in love, allowing love to go beyond mere information and become performative and transformative.

The Gospels tell us that one of the ways evil manifests itself is by preventing the word, blocking it. Jesus intervenes to heal the word because as we said earlier, when communication is affected through isolation, then one is truly defenceless.

For evil to act in our lives, it must first of all ruin channels of communication. We no longer mange to speak or listen. For example, when someone tells you what you must do to save yourself, what does evil do? It tells you about that individual's faults, and these become the tombstone which means you no longer listen. When we are alone, evil wins and we find ourselves being isolated from love which is communicated. When we do not feel loved, our worst side emerges and becomes diabolical. Desperate people do desperate things. Very often violence is the result of repressing our desperation, of our lack of love. Violence is communication with no human alphabet to say something.

Evil's winning argument is our misery: it is real, but it convinces us that the cause of our misery is that God does not love us, even when the Lord comes to tell us: 'I love you!' Our misery becomes an obstacle to our being loved by the Lord, creating something horrible in us that sounds like: 'To be loved you need to be free from your misery.' We will never free ourselves from our misery, at least in this life, so are we thus condemned to never feeling loved? God does not free us from our misery. God loves us in our misery. This is the experience of God's love; a God who loves us in our misery. 'God proves his love for us in that while we were still sinners, Christ died for us' (cf. Rom 5:8), but Zacchaeus and his story will tell us about that a little further on.

The gift of charity is the gift of the love the Father has for His Son. When this happens within us it becomes the foundation of our lives. Everything changes, everything becomes truly human. We can say that our life becomes liveable.

Without charity to give a foundation to our existence, our life is unliveable, poisonous, impractical. By reinterpreting everything with the key of 'being loved', it is as if we were saying that this is Commandment 0, zero being the prerequisite for all numbers to follow, including the first. When we allow ourselves to be loved, everything we do is done with inner joy, the joy of someone who knows that everything is possible, even loving, because we have first felt loved.

If we lose this perspective, that is, charity as the prerequisite, even the duty to love would not improve us. This is why the theological virtue of charity fundamentally means asking for such love.

In one of the Eucharistic prayers it says: 'You loved in us what you loved in the Son.' Here is the summary of everything we have said up till now. The Liturgy says it more succinctly and better. The gift of charity is knowing that God loves in us what he loves in the Son. When we ask him: 'Lord, give us the gift of charity' we are asking him for the love he has for the Son.

But, if it is true that the Father loves the Son, it is certainly true that the Son also loves the Father. This gift of love, a prerequisite for everything, this love of the Father, makes the Son's love well up in us. What significance does all this have? The fullness of love is allowing Christ to love in us, to respond to the father's love through us.

What motivates our life, our every choice? The fact that we feel we are doing something out of love, but not just any love, not simply our love. It is the awareness that it is the love of the Son within us. It is the Son who is loving at that moment, the Son who is responding to the Father's love. Truly loving means allowing the Son's love, not just any love, to well up in us.

St Paul puts it well in just a few words: 'The love of Christ urges us on' (2 Cor 5:14).

What is it that urges us on? What urges us on in our vocation? What urges us to do what we are doing? What gets us up in the morning? What urges us to pray? What urges us to make sacrifices? What is it that urges us to give our lives? The love of Christ urges us; we feel within this love the Son urging us to carry out this gesture. It is not the Son's love as a moral commandment but the Son's love as his own 'feeling.'

Spiritual maturity does not consist in doing what the Son commands us to do. That is simply the beginning of spiritual life. The fullness of spiritual life is doing things because in reality it is Christ's love in us that urges us on: 'Have the same mind as Jesus Christ.' It is as if Christ within us begins to gradually become our true motivation. This is the fullness of spiritual life.

This means that whatever we do it is the Son who does it. It is Jesus himself doing it. Who is praying? It is the Son who is praying. Who is celebrating Eucharist? It is the Son celebrating Eucharist. Who is it who gives his life for your children when you love them? It is Christ himself giving his life through you. Who is at work? Christ is at work. Who is it who sacrifices himself? It is Christ who sacrifices himself. We identify with the Son who has us say that we have made room in our spiritual life for Trinitarian love. What has lit this fire within us? This love that precedes us, the Father's love. What has produced the Father's love within us? The consequence of the Son's love is that we ourselves have become the Son. Until our gestures are those of the Son, until we understand that what we do is not us doing it but Christ himself working though us, spiritual life has not achieved its fullness in us, the fullness that made Christ say: 'The Father and I are one' (Jn 10:30).

Ours are always outward liturgies until we recognise individually that I am this Mass celebrated, I am the altar, victim and priest. In a word: I am the Son at that moment, and I have the greatest privilege of being crucified, of being more than ever the priest.

During the liturgy of ordination the bishop says: 'Conform yourself to what you are celebrating.' Here we are, then, and in certain moments of life we feel how true this call is, that we have taken on his very form. A moment of human failure, a moment of terrible human weakness makes us understand what it means for the Son to be present. This image is constantly put to us in the spiritual life – but it is a reality not simply an image, not just any 'form.'

The greatest spiritual maturity is allowing ourselves to be loved by the Father. The fullness of this spiritual life is allowing the Son in us to respond to this love.

When that happens, when you understand that as you experience illness, for example, it is the Son who is suffering, the essential nature of Trinitarian love is re-established.

The same Trinitarian love that was on Calvary becomes present at that moment. The Father returns to love the Son who usually feels alone and abandoned on the cross, but who says: 'I consign it all into your hands.' This dynamic is once again carried out within us. We do not repeat but conform to the single, unique occasion when Christ did all that.

Now, our entire life, every gesture of ours, every breath, every prayer, is the Son's prayer, the Son's love. It is the Son who is loving through us.

The range of miracles in the New Testament, at least as they are presented to us by John, begins with the miracle at the Wedding Feast at Cana. Mary tells the servants: 'Do whatever he tells you' (Jn 2:5). This is only the beginning.

At the beginning we do what Christ commands, but the aim is to become the Son. What is the aim of our Christian life? To become the Son and let Christ's love take possession of us every day that passes, to the point where it is the Son himself through me who lives, prays, loves, praises, suffers, gives.

> In the days of his flesh, Jesus offered up prayers and supplications, with loud cries and tears, to the one who was able to save him from death, and he was heard because of his reverent submission (Heb 5:7).

Jesus cries out aloud, asks to be freed and God hears him. I am no longer ashamed to cry out, to existentially take upon myself all the rebellions we find signs of in the Bible. In the greatest drama of our humanity all the humanity of the Son is manifested, the love of Christ in us. We can do nothing unless we are loved by the Father, but the Father's love is of no help if the response is not the Son's love.

It is simple to live our lives as servants and not as friends. It is simpler, but that is not our call.

One day, Jesus recounted the parable of the talents:

> For it is as if a man, going on a journey, summoned his slaves and entrusted his property to them; to one he gave five talents, to another two, to another one, to

each according to his ability. Then he went away. The one who had received the five talents went off at once and traded with them, and made five more talents. In the same way, the one who had received the one talent went off and dug a hole in the ground and hid his master's money. After a long time the master of those slaves came and settled accounts with them. Then the one who had received the five talents came forward, bringing five more talents, saying, 'Master, you handed over to me five talents; see, I have made five more talents.' His master said to him, 'Well done, good and trustworthy slave; you have been trustworthy in a few things, I will put you in charge of many things; enter into the joy of your master.' And the one with the two talents also came forward, saying, 'Master, you handed over to me two talents; see, I have made two more talents.' His master said to him, 'Well done, good and trustworthy slave; you have been trustworthy in a few things, I will put you in charge of many things; enter into the joy of your master.' Then the one who had received the one talent also came forward, saying, 'Master, I knew that you were a harsh man, reaping where you did not sow, and gathering where you did not scatter seed; so I was afraid, and I went and hid your talent in the ground. Here you have what is yours.' But his master replied, 'You wicked and lazy slave! You knew, did you, that I reap where I did not sow, and gather where I did not scatter? Then you ought to have invested my money with the bankers, and on my return I would have received what was my own with interest. So take the talent from him, and give it to the one with the ten talents. For to all those who have, more will be given, and they will have an abundance; but from those who have nothing, even what they have will be

> taken away. As for this worthless slave, throw him into the outer darkness, where there will be weeping and gnashing of teeth' (Mt 25:14–30).

What is wrong with the reasoning of the slave who hides his talent? In reality, if we reflect on it well, the slave is the only one who offers a sensible, astute reason among them. The others just take risks. One has ten, another five; 'I've only got one' thinks the man. 'If I lose it, it's all over for me. I will hide it, keep it untouched, and when he comes back I will return it to him.' There is reason here. What this slave thinks is reasonable. Most of the mistaken spiritual choices we make have perfect reasoning. Spiritual reasons are hardly even mathematical because they all have an element of risk to them. What is it that this slave has not understood? It is that the man in charge is giving him a talent so he can behave like him and not reason like a slave. He is meant to reason in terms of an investment: only an owner can invest, because he is an owner. But if the Father gives us something, it is not because he wants to keep what he gives. It is not talents he has at heart, but himself. He is not afraid of our sins, not afraid of the fact that we have never tried to risk our lives, never risked anything, because we are afraid of losing something. Maybe we have come to the end of our life all neat and tidy, but useless.

Once again, St Paul lends us the words to describe this passage: 'all belongs to you, and you belong to Christ, and Christ belongs to God' (1 Cor 3:22–23). This is the syllogism of salvation.

It is all ours, and we must live our life in a spirit of freedom, a law of freedom that comes from love. People who are unloved do not know how to be free. Only the one who is loved is free, and acts as a consequence.

When Paul says: 'For freedom Christ has set us free' (Gal 5:1) he is telling us that Christ has given us such love that it has made us free and we need to defend this freedom of ours.

I believe this may also be the reason why the prayer Jesus taught us begins with the word 'Abba,' Father. The prayer is letting Jesus say the word 'Father' within us.

Prayer is experience of the Father.

Prayer is allowing Jesus to give us the experience of the Father.

Prayer is not something we do but something Jesus does in us.

Prayer is Jesus saying 'Our Father' within us.

'And because you are children, God has sent the Spirit of his Son into our hearts, crying 'Abba! Father!" (Gal 4:6). This, then, is prayer.

Zacchaeus, or about free gift

The story of the conversion of a small, provincial 'Mafioso' called Zacchaeus can be helpful for exploring the logic of God's love:

> He entered Jericho and was passing through it. A man was there named Zacchaeus; he was a chief tax collector and was rich. He was trying to see who Jesus was, but on account of the crowd he could not, because he was short in stature. So he ran ahead and climbed a sycamore tree to see him, because he was going to pass that way. When Jesus came to the place he looked up and said to him, 'Zacchaeus, hurry and come down; for

> I must stay at your house today.' So he hurried down and was happy to welcome him. All who saw it began to grumble and said, 'He has gone to be the guest of one who is a sinner.'
>
> Zacchaeus stood there and said to the Lord, 'Look, half my possessions, Lord, I will give to the poor; and if I have defrauded anyone of anything, I will pay back four times as much.' Then Jesus said to him, 'Today salvation has come to this house, because he too is a son of Abraham. For the Son of Man came to seek out and to save the lost.' (Lk 19:1–10).

There is one characteristic of this man that helps us interpret his personality. He is short. When we have a handicap we always try to compensate for it with something else, meaning we develop an alternative way of staying afloat. Being small of stature can mean many things, as for example feeling we are beneath others. This inner ailment which we could describe as frustration (humility gone wrong) is the opposite to another inner pathology, pride, setting ourselves above others. Humility instead means being on equal terms with others.

Humility knows how to speak well of the self without pretending it is not the case. At the same time, humble people do not start believing things about themselves that are not true, like a cat showing its teeth pretending it is a lion, so it can scare off the other animal trying to scare it.

Humility consists in being on equal terms with self, others, God.

Humility is managing to look people in the eye without lowering our gaze.

It is very difficult for us to be on equal terms; very difficult to really be humble.

Similarly, perhaps to mark his frustration, I believe Zacchaeus develops a cunning, shrewd and dangerous side. He finds a fully human strategy for affirming himself over others. We also see this from the way he finds to overcome the obstacle of the crowd which prevents him from seeing Jesus; he climbs a sycamore tree. From the height of his cunning and shrewdness, however, he wants to see the Lord and this is another very interesting piece of information: however bad in whatever sense we might become, we still have a desire within to see the Lord.

Even the worst people want to be happy. Even the worst people want to find meaning in their lives. Not even Zacchaeus, who certainly would have been better than me, is absolved from this desire. He feels it, notices it, finds a strategy of his own and up he climbs. The sycamore is his technique for staying afloat, overcoming his shortness. The proud man is always the frustrated one in reverse. Jesus passes by and the Gospel tells us: 'he looked up and said to him, "Zacchaeus, hurry and come down, for I must stay at your house today."' It is Jesus who looks up at him. It is Jesus who notices him. Zacchaeus would have simply been happy to be a spectator of the scene, to watch Jesus pass by without being called by name. The real experience of conversion consists precisely in this: conversion is not recognising Christ or a truth, or the meaning of life, but hearing oneself being called by name by this Truth and this Meaning.

Initially, it seems that Jesus does not know how to sell his image well. One does not win over the people by coming to a new town and dining with the local Mafia! Jesus is not afraid to risk losing face out of love for Zacchaeus. We can imagine the comments: 'Here's another one, another word merchant who has immediately worked out the house where the money is.' Jesus completely loses his reputation, his name, any grasp on being thought credible in Jericho's eyes, and all for what? For love of Zacchaeus. We could end the story here. We would mistakenly go on with the story, thinking it was all about strategies. But the truth is this: why does Jesus love Zacchaeus? So he will convert? No. He loves him, full stop.

Christ's love is free, since he asks nothing in return, not even our conversion. Christ loves us not so we become better persons – he loves us even if we decide not to. This is the scandal of God's love, the scandal of God's freely given love. God's love is not of the shrewd kind that says: 'I will give you something but you have to behave!' No. It is: 'I will give you this. That's all. I'm not looking for anything. Do you wish to keep on behaving badly? I will continue loving you. I love you even in your sins.'

'All who saw it began to grumble and said, "He has gone to be the guest of one who is a sinner." Zacchaeus stood there and said, "Look, half my possessions, Lord, I will give to the poor; and if I have defrauded anyone of anything I will pay back four times as much."' Jesus did not ask him to do this. It was Zacchaeus who decided to. His conversion certainly comes from an encounter, but one that leaves him free to make the decision to change. He is not under pressure from a business exchange. There is no strategic feeling of guilt aroused in him. We cannot become better people when urged on by a feeling of guilt because Jesus loved us. For too long we have held up the crucifix saying: 'Since he died because of your fault, then the least you can do is to behave properly.' This is a mistake. Christ did not go to the cross to arouse guilt in us so we would change our life. 'I will love you even if you never change, even if you always reject me, even if you decide to give nothing, to continue being a tax collector. I will love you to the extent of dying for you, always, just because you do not deserve it; none of us deserves love.' None of us. Christ's love cannot be bought, it is freely given. It is this freely given love that provokes the freedom in us to decide to do good, or not feel constrained to do something good.

Christ died for us when we were still sinners. Christ died for us when we deserved nothing.

None of us can decide to change our life because we feel guilty, but we can do it because we decide to be a different person. Perhaps we decide to be a different person. Perhaps we decide after a decisive encounter, but it is still we who decide. It is not the fear of hell that makes us better people. Perhaps it can make us behave better, but it will not have changed our heart. This is why Jesus says: 'Today, salvation has come to this house,' because love was freely accepted by Zacchaeus through an act of freedom which was a break with his past.

God's love is a disinterested love. It is interesting, fascinating, but not interested in the utilitarian sense.

God does not love us in such a way that we then need to give something in return. He loves us and that is enough.

The decision to be better people is up to our freedom. The fact that at a certain point we begin to live better does not come from fear of punishment, but from a much deeper freedom aroused by an awareness that someone loves us this way.

Too many of our conversions are the result of guilt feelings and thus they often come to a quick end, because guilt feelings tend to go up and down. When we feel guilty we behave well, and when we forget our guilt we return to being the people we were before.

'God's love is in me because I am behaving well.' Instead the truth is that we are a temple of the Holy Spirit even when we are the worst people in the world: 'Or do you not know that your body is a temple of the Holy Spirit within you, which you have from God, and that you are not your own?' (1 Cor 6:19).

Someone said: 'What difference is there between someone who believes in God's love and someone who instead rejects it? Nothing. Only that the former enjoys life more!' The fact of rejecting God's love does not take God's love from us; we simply do not enjoy life, can't savour it, because we are deliberately living as if that love did not exist.

The truth is that nothing can separate us from the love of Christ:

> What then are we to say about these things? If God is for us, who can be against us? He who did not withhold his own Son, but gave him up for all of us, will he not with him also give us everything else? Who will bring any charge against God's elect? It is God who justifies. Who is to condemn? It is Christ Jesus, who died, yes, who was raised, who is at the right hand of God, who indeed intercedes for us. Who will separate us from the love of Christ? Will hardship, or distress, or persecution, or famine, or nakedness, or peril or sword? As it is written, 'For your sake we are being killed all day long; we are accounted as sheep to be slaughtered.' No, in all these things we are more than conquerors through him who loved us. For I am

> convinced that neither death nor life, nor angels, nor rulers, nor things present, nor things to come, nor powers, nor height, nor depth, nor anything else in all creation, will be able to separate us from the love of God in Christ Jesus our Lord. (Rom 8:31–39).

How does one end up in hell? By a free, conscious act, one that deliberately rejects this love. I don't think I am speaking heresy if I state that we can also decide to set ourselves against God's love and turn everything into hell and go there for eternity, but we cannot stop God from continuing to love us. We are free not to accept it but we cannot stop our being loved.

No one can say: 'I went and ended up in hell because the Lord took his love away from me.' The Lord can never take his love from us, because He has always freely loved us. He has never asked us for anything, not even our conversion. He has loved us and that's it. He has loved us and left us free to respond and correspond, or not, to this love.

This is why we can approach the sacraments and immediately afterwards have the freedom to commit some terrible misdeed.

How come the power of the sacrament does not stop me from doing this? Because God's grace does not paralyse our freedom. It is this that makes us doubly responsible for what we do.

We should allow ourselves to be re-educated by the freedom of God's love. When we feel we are freely loved we allow ourselves to be transformed by that love.

It is a sin not to acknowledge that he wants to love us. It is a sin not to acknowledge that the Father loves us. It is a sin not to let Jesus be able to love the Father within us.

Instead, when we do allow it we become like Mary. Mary is transparent. This Trinitarian love in her is perfect. Being immaculate means she is no obstacle to this love.

Instead, our ego is sometimes like a huge stone blocking this flow: the Father's love crashes against our ego but does not manage to dislodge it, meaning we do not allow the Son to respond. We smother the Son in us.

When we do not love, we are stopping Christ from loving.

Maturity in spiritual life is allowing Christ to love in us!

4

Freedom to Breathe

(Or how the Spirit leaves his mark)

> The wind blows where it chooses, and you hear the sound of it, but you do not know where it comes from or where it goes. So it is of everyone who is born of the Spirit (Jn 3:8).

To understand how the Spirit acts we have sought to understand the dynamics of faith, hope and charity in our life.

Every time we leave room for these gifts of God in us, the Spirit is at work in us and room for freedom is created. It is room for God's freedom.

God breathes his freedom into us, hence Jesus tells Nicodemus that the Spirit blows where he wills like the wind.

There is a radical freedom created in the human heart when we allow it to be inhabited by God's love. It is as if the human being were torn away from his or her determinism, no longer the simple product of action and reaction. The human being becomes fully image and likeness of God.

What is it that brings about this full likeness to God? Freedom. One of the most important goals of our life is to recover our inner freedom.

What does it mean, for example, for someone suffering from cancer to recover their inner freedom? Is it to get well? No, but to get to the point of understanding that 'I am not my cancer.' I might have cancer but I am not my cancer.

When I succeed in making this distinction between me and my illness, I have recovered room for freedom. This makes me like God. The spiritual life is as if we have created these cushions of space in us. It helps us distinguish. You can see someone with cancer living with extraordinary inner freedom even though it does not spare him the humiliation of illness, the pain, suffering, even death. The Spirit is at work in this person, meaning God's freedom is at work, and what should only be death, and a fearful death among other things, becomes sanctification.

Our real problem is this: it is not enough to simply be alive, not enough to simply do what we have to do. What makes saints of us is doing what we have to do with inner freedom. If we do not have inner freedom to act, even to make a sacrifice, a choice, then that sacrifice and choice does not make us saints. Holiness is savouring the joy of life, an inner certainty that nothing we are going through is useless, even if it is apparently so.

Only the Spirit enables what the Spirit is asking. God asks something of us and it is God himself who makes us capable of that something he asks of us. Our drama and what makes us real, is that faced with the requests of the Spirit we feel so incapable, as if it all depended on us. Until we see that the huge thing the Lord is asking of us is made possible by him, then his requests will always be a drama for us.

What is spiritual renewal then? It is not a change of habit, of clothing, not a change of *habitus*, our habits.

Someone might say: 'We are renewed because we have renewed our Rule, or renewed our plans for each day, the way we live together eat, pray, work.' But spiritual renewal has nothing to do with our habits. Spiritual renewal is a change of heart not of clothing, because we could also change our clothing (rules, house, friends, gestures, prayers…) but still be wolves in sheep's clothing. Indeed, we become more dangerous. James Joyce, an outstanding writer, once said: 'I do not fear the wolf's bites, but the sheep's,' and I add that I fear even more the bites of wolves in sheep's clothing.

Spiritual renewal is a change of heart and we are called to this. If we want to let the Spirit act within us we must let the Lord carry out what he himself says in the Word: 'I will remove from your body the heart of stone and give you a heart of flesh' (Ezek 36:26).

Our problem is always the same: hardness of heart, the fact that over time, even if we are men and women of God, believers, even if we are constantly in touch with the sacred, with his presence, our heart hardens. We suffer from this illness of hardness of heart, or better put, hardening of heart. Our heart becomes stone. We need, then, for the Lord to work a change in us; take away our heart of stone and give us a new heart of flesh.

At times, the heart of stone comes because we can no longer put up with things. It is a kind of defence, a protection.

If we are not doing well in a situation, the only way we have to tackle the difficulty is to find a very human strategy, which often coincides with taking our distance from things. We do not have a heart of stone because we were born that way. I have never yet met people who are radically bad –

who have become radically bad. In Italian the word '*cattivo*' (bad) comes from the Latin *captivus* meaning a captive, a slave. So in this sense the bad person is a slave, and there are things in life which enslave us, place us, in a situation of slavery. This slavery brings out the worst in us.

I am not interested in why we have a heart of stone; perhaps as defence, to survive or we have done so out of pure malice. We can never really say with certainty. What we do know for sure is that the Lord is the only one who can take out our heart of stone and give us a heart of flesh, and that a change of clothing is no help at all unless we change heart, unless we let the Lord change our heart. The most extraordinary thing about spiritual renewal is that the Lord replaces the spirit of the world which normally blows within us, with the Spirit of Pentecost, the Spirit of the Risen Lord.

In place of the worldly spirit we all bear within, the Lord gives us another Spirit, his! Without Pentecost nothing is possible. Peter's repentance is no help, not even the experience of the Risen Lord helps without the experience of Pentecost.

For weeks, the disciples touch, eat with, speak with the Risen Lord and despite that remain locked away. One can attend Mass and still be closed off: change is not automatic. It is not said that since we have touched the Risen Lord, eaten with him, made Eucharist with him, this automatically pulls us away from the Upper Room where we have locked ourselves in. It can seem frustrating: What can we do if not even Jesus Christ can pull us out of here, if not even his presence can pull us out of where we have been hunted to? Who will save us? Only the experience of Pentecost, that something more that comes from God: the Spirit of the

Risen Lord. And this is because we do have fears, moments of isolation, insecurities in us which are invincible.

There are the kinds of fears whereby no matter how you reason with them, there seems no way out. You can't handle it. There are times when we shut ourselves off and there seems to be no way to overcome it; we are reeling, and perhaps a friend tells us: 'Trust me, I will give you a hand.' I may so much want to trust this person. My head says 'trust you' but in fact I cannot manage to do so, as if my will were effectively paralysed.

What keeps the disciples shut away in the Upper Room is something larger than they are. So only something larger than them can free them, since the Risen Lord has no problem entering through locked doors. Christ is not afraid of our locked doors, our fears, insecurities; not our sins, which are other ways of closing ourselves off.

He comes through locked doors.

The problem is not Christ entering. The problem is that I don't go out. The difficulty of conversion is not in saying: 'I don't manage to let Jesus into my life.' We cannot say this because Jesus enters our life through locked doors. The problem is that it is we who do not go out. There is no actual change in us, just the desire, and sometimes not even that. I think the disciples too, at a certain point, wanted out of there but could not. It is then that the Spirit breaks through, forcibly flings open the doors:

> When the day of Pentecost had come, they were all together in one place. And suddenly from heaven there came a sound like the rush of a violent wind, and it filled the entire house where they were sitting. Divided tongues as of fire, appeared among them. All

> of them were filled with the Holy Spirit and began to speak in other languages, as the Spirit gave them ability (Acts 2:1–4).

If spiritual renewal is a change of heart, it is one that only the Lord can bring about. This personal and communal change of heart is the experience of Pentecost.

Can any of us make Pentecost happen? No, no one has the power to say: 'Now is the moment for Pentecost.' This too is God's gift. But we can prepare ourselves to welcome the moment, as for it. Our part in spiritual renewal is to prepare for Pentecost, ask for this Pentecost, ready ourselves for it. How do we do this?

The first thing to prepare for Pentecost is a most important element. Let us be assisted by events as we know them from the Gospels and the Acts of the Apostles. Initially the difficulties of Jesus' arrest, passion, death, divide the disciples. We all know there are so many valid reasons, in every setting, for division. However, after the initial division arising from their difficulty and the knowledge that initially they are divided because confused, the disciples become a compact group once more – because they decide to. If it is true that communion is God's gift it is also true that what precedes it, what prepares for communion with God and between us, is the fact that we decide to unite once more. We make a deliberate choice to.

There can be no Pentecost if personally and as a community we do not make the decision to be together, think together, recognise that our destiny is inexorably bound up with that of our brothers and sisters. We cannot think things through on our own. We need to do it with others, difficult though it may be. The first thing that prepares for Pentecost is to reassemble the ranks through a precise decision. Theology says that the decisions that count are called 'fundamental options.' We need to go back to the fundamental option of being together. If we want to save a broken family the very first thing to do is not seek help or ask God's help, but ask ourselves if we still want to decide to be a family. Then we can ask help from God and others.

Beyond this relationship, this togetherness, there is no salvation. The first thing we need to do for our renewal, and maybe for the renewal of the whole world, is to achieve the fundamental option of seeing ourselves as a body, where our destiny is absolutely bound up with that of our brothers and sisters, that it is not possible to do our thinking alone without thinking of their good.

People are not just responsible for themselves but also for those around them. Otherwise it is the primordial refusal of Cain, who after killing his brother Abel, tries to hide his crime by saying to God: 'Am I my brother's keeper?' (Gen 4:9).

The only way to get to the top of an alpine peak is by being roped together. One does not get far alone on such a mountain. It is by being roped together that the ascent is enabled. What makes holiness possible is the Church. What makes it possible to fully achieve our destiny, is being together. Certainly there are times when we want to say: 'I would like to do without Tom, Dick, Harry, I would like a promotion, some distance from the group, some recognition.' But no matter how much this can give us some psychological relief, we need to know that only together, which is the Church for a believer, is our holiness possible.

So, the first thing that allows Pentecost to happen is to be roped together again, to choose to do so. We need to exorcise isolation and solipsism.

The second preparatory feature for Pentecost is a direct suggestion from Acts: 'All these were constantly devoting themselves to prayer, together with certain women including Mary, the mother of Jesus, as well as his brothers' (Acts 1:14).

This is returning to prayer. Not just regular prayer, but as the text says '…constantly…together…' With one heart. In the living tradition of the Church we discover extraordinary, almost unexpected assistance from Gregorian Chant. Gregorian Chant is an exercise in concord, unison out of diversity. The Gregorian melody has us rising, falling, performing virtuosity with the voice. It spins out vocal passages at great length and urges a musical performance such that inevitably it sounds like a single voice singing. We do not hear the individual, just the single voice descending, moving, dancing. I like to think that the real aim of Gregorian is precisely this: an experience of bringing us into concord, bringing us together. The potential that comes from Gregorian lies in tapping into a way in return to being of one heart. This means that in order to be in unison with the other, we need to listen: your voice must be neither louder nor softer – one thing, unison, although we are many.

If it is true and possible for Gregorian, it is also true and possible for everyday life. To return to unison we have to start listening again. My heart, my person must be neither louder nor softer than those around me. Our life calls on virtuosity as in Gregorian. At times it calls on us to ascend to the heights, at times to descend to the depths, but it asks us to do it together, and this is a form of training. This is what is asked of our freedom.

Here, then, are the first two features; the first is the fundamental option of coming back together, roping ourselves together, closing ranks while the second is learning once more to be constant and of one heart, in concord.

It might be simpler for me to do everything alone. But 'easy' is not synonymous with 'effective.'

A third feature: 'All these were constantly devoting themselves to prayer...including Mary, the mother of Jesus.' This is another important thing to for us: Mary's presence. Too often Mary's presence in our life is a devotional, decorative one. For Pentecost instead her presence was decisive, not devotional. In the communion of saints this woman's presence is strictly tied to the destiny of every baptised member, every community, and it is very important for Pentecost to happen. It is not written explicitly in the Acts of the Apostles but I like to imagine that the opening, the crack through which the Spirit breaks in is Mary. She is the filter. Maybe for a very simple reason: she had already experienced the work of the Spirit on the day of the Annunciation.

We need to rethink Mary's presence in our life. She received an expansion of her calling beneath the cross:

> Meanwhile standing near the cross of Jesus were his mother, and his mother's sister, Mary the wife of Clopas, and Mary Magdalene. When Jesus saw his mother and the disciple whom he loved standing beside her, he said to his mother, 'Woman, here is your son.' Then he said to the disciple, 'Here is your

> mother.' And from that hour the disciple took her into his own home (Jn 19:25–27).

Beneath the cross, Mary is no longer only the Mother of Jesus, the Mother God according to the beautiful definition given us by the Council of Ephesus. Beneath the cross, Mary also becomes the Mother of John and hence of each of us. Mary is interested in us by vocation, not just as a pastime. The sooner we recognise that this woman's motherhood is given to us to make life even more possible and so we can live the good news of the Gospel, the sooner we will discover the correct and most welcoming position for receiving the gift of the Spirit.

Mary's absence makes us less attractive. Mary brings us a fundamental beauty. It is a little bit like when we were little, our mothers sent us off to school all neat and tidy. We felt we were looked after by someone. At times our communities are not particularly beautiful places because we have overlooked Mary and her motherliness. Or worse, we treat her as merely devotional, with a decorative impact, not a decisive existential one.

The fourth feature we find in a detail of the Pentecost account given us in Acts of the Apostles: 'And suddenly from heaven there came a sound like the rush of a violent wind, and it filled the entire house where they were sitting' (Acts 2:2). This is a power greater than the disciples' division and reference, Why is it important to be aware of this extraordinary power of the Holy Spirit? Because there inevitably comes a moment when personally or as a community we are a bit down, and we begin to say: 'How do we get out of this mess? Who will free us of all this?' The

Pentecost account tells us there is something even stronger than our depression, our sense of resignation, our inability.

> When the day of Pentecost had come, they were all together in one place. And suddenly from heaven there came a sound like the rush of a violent wind, and it filled the entire house where they were sitting. Divided tongues, as of fire, appeared among them, and a tongue rested on each of them. All of them were filled with the Holy Spirit and began to speak in other languages, as the Spirit gave them ability (Acts 2:1–4).

The spiritual sensation is that at a certain point something breaks through. It is typical of the Lord. What we always have been waiting for arrives when we least expect it. This is why everything is a sacrament for us. It is real, it points to something. The person beside me is a sacrament for me, a real person, but at the same time points to my Father in heaven. There is something stronger than our efforts to close ourselves off.

Then there is the gift of tongues. Our reticence and withdrawal creates confusion, inability to understand, we speak different languages. We then suffer from what we call the syndrome of misunderstanding. No one understands me. No one suffers like I do. No one feels like I do. Worse still is being convinced that I cannot communicate just how I feel. Pentecost contains within it the experience of understanding one another: they 'began to speak in other languages, as the Spirit gave them ability'; and further on:

> Amazed and astonished, they asked, 'Are not all these who are speaking Galileans? And how is it that we

> hear, each of us, in our own native language? Parthians, Medes, Elamites, and residents of Mesopotamia, Judea and Cappodocia, Pontus and Asia, Phrygia and Pamohilia, Egypt and the parts of Libya belonging to Cyrene, and visitors from Rome, both Jews and proselytes, Cretans and Arabs – in our own languages we hear them speaking about God's deeds of power.' All were amazed and perplexed, saying to one another, 'What does this mean?' (Acts 2:7–12).

There is one final feature: Pentecost helps us reinterpret wisely our personal and community experience. Peter reinterprets his betrayal and repentance this way; so do the disciples wisely reinterpret their experience with Jesus, their running away and their return to be a single group.

The gift of spiritual renewal makes us understand the link with the past and does not allow any overlooking of the past. When we sometimes think of the present, or what God is doing in the present as a break with the past, it means we think God has begun to work now but not earlier, and so claim that the present is always better than the past. As a consequence we claim we are better today than we were in the past. Even within the Church we have come to create a certain erroneous mentality of the kind. Especially during the beautiful post-conciliar flourishing that followed Vatican II, the idea spread that the Council had wrought a real transformation of quality, as if to say: we are better than those who came before us. The truth of the Council is extraordinary because there was no break, but a wiser interpretation of the Church's living Tradition. Fracture brought injury, not flourishing. I was struck on one occasion, reading Antonio Gramschi's *Quaderni dal carcere*

(Prison Notebooks): 'A generation which puts the previous generation down can only be petty... By devaluing the past it is implicitly a justification of the invalidity of the present.'

The wise interpretation is to understand that there is a Providence linking everything, what comes before with what comes after, the past with the present. If we are here, it is because we are the children of a past which we cannot disown. But a contradictory element is also true: being children of a past means recovering an originality in the present. The beauty of the saints lies in the fact that they were who they were at that moment. The highest imitation of the saints is their originality, their inimitability. It is as if they were constantly telling us: 'Do as we did. Do not imitate us,' that is, don't simply repeat what you have already seen but starting with that, be new, unique, original.

We look at the past to say we must have the courage to take on this moment in history as unique and unrepeatable, and have the courage to be ourselves at this historical moment, to say the same thing but in a different way. It is not just playing with words. It is about renewal because it is always going back to the roots, to what is essential in things.

By vocation we are constantly called to return to the roots, to what is essential in everything.

How does this manifest itself today? I do not know. This is discernment and touches on us all as individuals and a community. What does it mean for us to live this vocation today?

Spiritual renewal, Pentecost, recreates profound unity between Heaven and Earth, between Heaven and our brothers and sisters. 'Just as you did it to them you did it to me' (cf. Mt 25). The first worship of God is love for our brothers and sisters. It is the first liturgy we are called to celebrate. As experts in this liturgy we render worship to God firstly by loving our brothers and sisters. 'Those who do not love a brother or a sister whom they have seen, cannot love God whom they have not seen' (cf. 1 Jn 4:20). For me, the other person is essential: he or she is the substance of what I believe.

The brother, sister you see

Our faith always revolves around the flesh of our brothers and sisters. Even a hermit has to deal with the flesh of his brothers and sisters because solitude is never isolation. Isolation is an infernal condition. Solitude is a condition of exclusivity, intimacy. One chooses solitude out of love, love for one's brothers and sisters, hence love of God. Or, out of love of God, hence love of our brothers and sisters. We are always bound together. St Paul is right when he tells us we are one body: 'So we, who are many are one body in Christ and individually we are members one of another' (Rom 12:5).

Our greatest effort is to understand how to tie our spiritual worship to the worship the Lord asks us to render to him, by loving our brothers and sisters. When these two dimensions are opposed, that is when we go under. It is like someone with indigestion. Something is blocked, not digested. Personal and community short circuits occur at times when we fail to hold spiritual worship and love for our brothers and sisters together. The proof of our intimacy with God is the charity we experience with our brothers and sisters:

> Whoever says, 'I am in the light,' while hating a brother or sister, is still in darkness. Whoever loves a brother or sister lives in the light, and in such a person there is no cause for stumbling. But whoever hates another believer is in the darkness, walks in the darkness, and does not know the way to go, because the darkness has bought on blindness (1 Jn 2:9–11).

When I think of this, I am aware that I am still far from the goal. I might certainly have the grace to understand many truths, know how to put them into words, explain them to others, but what counts is not the clarity of my reasoning and words. The authentically spiritual person loves. The real question is not how clear our ideas are, but why we do not manage to forgive a mother, father, friend. It is because I haven't forgiven the person who made me suffer. Care and passion for things that never give us something in exchange.

When we suffer, or hate someone because they have wounded us, we think the best thing is to put some distance between us. We do not see, for example, that hatred is something very close to love. The real malady is not hatred but indifference. If you hate you can still be on the right path because hatred is always love gone wrong; it speaks of pain, failed relationship, but is at least relationship. Paradoxically there is still hope when there is hatred. But when we feel nothing, then the problem is serious.

So we should not be fearful if our relationships also include a slice of suffering. Rapport not only with my brothers and sisters who live with me, rapport with my history, with what has been the story of my life, perhaps brings me suffering but that simply says we are normal, we are human. It means there is nothing that should frighten us.

Let us look at three psalms that can help us speak some truth about ourselves.

Psalm 126

When the LORD restored the fortunes of Zion,
we were like those who dream.
Then our mouth was filled with laughter,
and our tongue with shouts of joy;
then it was said among the nations,
'The LORD has done great things for them.'
The LORD has done great things for us,
and we rejoiced.
Restore our fortunes O LORD,
like the watercourses in the Negeb.
May those who sow in tears
reap with shouts of joy.
Those who go out weeping,
bearing the seed for sowing,
shall come home with shouts of joy,
carrying their sheaves.

When we have spent long periods in an exile of desolation or problems and the Lord leads us back, it seems like a dream to us. Good always seems an illusion to us. We do not manage to immediately believe in good. It is as if it were a dream we will wake up from. But when we realise we are already awake, we are open-mouthed in surprise and our tongue loosens in songs of joy. It is not a joy of emotions but the joy of someone who understands that 'those who go out weeping will come home with shouts of joy.' There is a profound link between my tears and the harvest. Tears are the proof that there exists a harvest in joy. The good news of Christ is that our suffering is not in vain, that what we have gone through that causes us pain is not futile. God is the only one able to build bridges between tears and joy, between the tears of those who sow and the joy of those who reap. It does not say that we will be the ones to reap, but it is certain that our tears will not be wasted. Our suffering is never in vain. If it were, the Lord would take it from us. If he does not intervene it is because he has the capacity to build bridges with a harvest that we may touch on certain occasions, and indirectly on other occasions.

We need to have the courage to plant a tree knowing that perhaps we will enjoy nothing of what we have planted, not even the scent. One day, in a hundred years time, someone going along that road will enjoy the freshness of that tree.

That does not make me sad. It fills me with joy, because it is as if the Lord had given me the grace to understand in an instant that what I do now, and what apparently and immediately brings no result, certainly will at some stage. Someone else will enjoy it as I enjoy things thanks to those who have sown before me. It is a solid chain of love, where very often the love I put in will be enjoyed by someone other than me, since the love I enjoy comes form someone before me. Theology calls this link 'the communion of saints', and this is the importance of joy, its true substance.

Psalm 127

Unless the Lord builds the house,
those who build it labour in vain.
Unless the Lord guards the city,
the guards keep watch in vain.
It is in vain that you rise up early
and go late to rest,
eating the bread of anxious toil;
for he gives sleep to his beloved.

Sons are indeed a heritage from the Lord,
the fruit of the womb a reward.
Like arrows in the hand of a warrior
are the sons of one's youth.
Happy the man who has
his quiver full of them.
He shall not be put to shame
when he speaks with his enemies in the gate.

We could describe this psalm as the Magna Carta of Christian awareness: 'Unless the Lord builds the house, those who build it labour in vain.' It sounds simple, but it is the thing we forget most often. Unless the Lord does the building all our efforts and work are in vain. The primacy of God in our life. Every healthy spiritual renewal is evangelised by this psalm. So what do we need to do? Let him do the building. When you let him do the building you arm yourself with patience and peace because his times are not yours. Arm yourself with listening, because maybe his thoughts are not your thoughts 'My ways are not your ways.' This is very reassuring for us because 'Unless the Lord guards the city, the guard keeps watch in vain.' Stress, ulcers catch up with us because we want to control the house, and when we realise everything is collapsing day by day, we fall ill. But you are not the builder or the guard. Relax! If you think it is up to you, then you rise in vain of a morning and go to bed late in vain, and in vain do you eat the bread you have sweated for. Do you know what the Lord does? He gives bread to his friends while they sleep. It is as if we had spent a long time standing there propping up a load-bearing wall saying: 'If I move, the wall will collapse,' while the Lord says: 'Let go of it.' If you listen to him you will see that the wall stands up without you. How much time you have wasted glued to that wall to hold it up. We could have gone for a walk, spoken, enjoyed ourselves, but instead we spend years propping up load-bearing walls because we are inwardly convinced that this is our fundamental task and that we are essential and necessary to it. We are all valuable and important, all of us. But none of us is essential, only God.

Psalm 128

Happy is everyone who fears the LORD,
who walks in his ways.
You shall eat the fruit of the labour of your hands.
You shall be happy, and it shall go well with you.

Your WIFE will be like a fruitful vine
within your house;
Your children will be like olive shoots
around your table.
Thus shall the man be blessed
who fears the LORD

The LORD bless you from Zion.
May you see the prosperity of Jerusalem
all the days of your life.
May you see your children's children.
Peace be upon Israel!

There is always fruitfulness hidden in our true vocation. Love is always relationship, and the olive shoots are always the blessing the Lord gives us. The deepest honesty we should have in our own regard is to ask ourselves always what fruit we bear. Fruit, not results; quality, not quantity. There is a more important and significant fruit of all that speaks of the rightness of our life and choices: joy.

There is one thing that says we are truly Christians. There is a testimony that says our life is truly grafted onto Christ. After all we have said up to now, the answer should be: charity. But even more so we should say that charity has its splendour. The splendour of charity is joy.

This is the reason why we should ask ourselves; Do those who see us see our joy? Perhaps they see the penitent person, the serious individual, the friendly, conscientious human being, but do they see the joy? Because joy is the authentic test of all that is true in us.

Joy is not the absence of problems. True joy is something that is based on the Cross. Joy is a splendour that exists not because there are no problems, limitations, poverty, worries, but because despite all this, despite our limitations, our sin, problems, wounds, we are joyful. The joy Christ gives us is not the same joy that the world gives us. Christ does not give us joy by freeing us from the cross. He gives us joy in the cross because he gives us the joy of knowing we are loved when everything is very difficult. Our testimony is not to act in such a way that we are free of problems, wounds, sins, believing it is because of this that we will be joyful and become good witnesses to it. The truth is that we should be recognising quite the opposite. If this joy exists it is now, not tomorrow, because it does not depend on our merits. It does not depend on how good we have become. Instead it depends on the fact that I love him and am loved by him now; that I love him and am loved as I am. Whatever can happen to us or is happening now, no one can take the joy from us, this joy, this certainty. If there is something we must protect in our personal and community life, it is joy. We should learn to make an examination of conscience just on joy, ask ourselves how much joy is in us.

I believe that the truest test of holiness, the most beautiful testimony of holiness is joy. Not the joy of eternally fixed smiles but joy as a light emanating from us, from our eyes especially, and from the tenderness with which we deal with life.

This is why joy has much to do with one word: peace. Peace of heart. Peace which is not just the absence of conflict.

Let us allow ourselves to be helped by a passage from Mark's Gospel:

> On that day, when evening had come, he said to them, 'Let us go across to the other side.' And leaving the crowd behind, they took him with them in the boat, just as he was. Other boats were with him, A great windstorm arose, and the waves beat into the boat so that the boat was already being swamped. But he was in the stern, asleep on the cushion; and they woke him up and said to him, 'Teacher, do you not care that we are perishing?' He woke up and rebuked the wind, and said to the sea, 'Peace! Be still!' Then the wind ceased, and there was a dead calm. He said to them, 'Why are you afraid? Have you still no faith?' And they were filled with great awe and said to one another, 'Who then is this, that even the wind and the sea obey him?' (Mk 4:35–41).

Jesus is in the boat. There is a storm. He is asleep. This already tells us a lot; how is it possible for a storm to be threatening and he is asleep and doesn't wake up? This is precisely the perception we have at times of Jesus. We can enter a church, approach the tabernacle and feel as if faith is telling us he is there, but also have the feeling that he is asleep compared to what we are actually going through. 'Rouse yourself! Why do you sleep, O Lord? Awake, do not cast us off forever!' (Ps 44:23). The Gospel tells us; Jesus is there, really there, but asleep. So what do the disciples do? Initially they try not to disturb him and row with their own strength. But despite every effort and strength they put into it the storm seems to have the upper hand. Finally they go to the stern, just as we at times go up to the tabernacle: 'Do you not care that we are perishing?' Jesus finally wakes up, and what does he do? 'He rebukes the wind, and said to the sea 'Peace! Be still!' Then the wind ceased and there was a dead calm. He said to them, 'Why are you afraid? Have you still no faith?'' This is our problem. Inevitably at a certain point we believe more in the storm than in Jesus being in our boat. This is how our real lack of faith shows up: the storms become more important than his presence. What is it the disciples do not grasp at that moment? And that we do not grasp? We can also believe Jesus is asleep but it is the appalling suggestion of fear: 'Do you not care that we are perishing?' As St Paul puts it: 'He who did not withhold his own Son but gave him up for all of us, will he not with him give us everything else?' (Rom 8:32).

Every particle of your life matters to the one who gave his life for you. So why does he allow the storms? I don't know.

I don't know why certain things happen, I don't know why at times we find ourselves in absurd situations. I don't know what unleashes the storms. I don't know why He is there but asleep. I don't know how to reply to the question. I know just one thing for certain – that He is there. This gives me peace. This is my strength: knowing He is there and while this is so, all goes well. Paradoxically, it all goes well even if we drown! 'By you I can crush a troop and by my God I can leap over a wall' (Ps 18:29).

When you go to war and you know you are alone against ten thousand, it would be normal to think you will lose. But a Christian recognises this as knowing how to lose. We do not always win; there is not always a solution to things, and at times holiness consists in knowing how to lose. For sure the time will come in life when we do lose: our death. How should our faith view this? Not from the perspective that the Lord will intervene at some stage and we will no longer die, but from the perspective of how we lose faced with death, because we know that even there we are never alone.

This is what makes it possible to face up to everything. The same goes for any occasion when death shows up in our life through death – dealing with difficult, unforeseen and incomprehensible circumstances. How should any Christianity, any faith, see itself then? From the position I take in the storm. Explaining storms does nothing to remove all the drama of the storm.

The Church has gone through a period when it was held hostage somewhat to sociological investigation. Sociological analysis was carried out to understand why people were not attending Mass. But how many people did these sociological analyses bring back? Not one. An explanation of the storm is not also a solution to it. We should not fossilise ourselves too much in analysis but focus on the stance we want to take before a problem; the worst we can do is to never take a stance before things, put things off or worse, become fatalistic. Fatalism is a visual error (how I look at matters) which has us say that the meaning of things lies in a reason I am being subjected to, and in the final analysis, it becomes the explanation and maybe also the scapegoat. We are all capable of taking an event and turning it to what pleases us. The daily horoscopes always do this because they more or less say: 'Today will be a wonderful day, but it also may not be.' This is fatalism: taking bits and pieces of events and reassembling them in such a way that they tell us what we want to hear. Instead of wasting time with spiritual horoscopes we should get on with taking a stance before things.

What is the best stance?

Mary's and Joseph of Nazareth's.

We have already spoken of Mary and understand why. But Joseph?

I would like to pause for a moment to reflect on the extraordinary beauty of this figure.

Joseph is a man who, like all others, has expectations for his life. He too would have worked out in his head a rough plan for being happy. What is wrong with wanting a wife and children? I think being in love is a very beautiful thing, yet God enters this man's life asking him to renounce his dreams and embrace His instead. God responds to this man's desire for fatherhood by not making him a father according to the flesh but by asking him to be a 'foster father' in place of another. His entire life could look like continual acceptance of everything he didn't want. There is not a single word of his recorded in the Gospel. This man is the true image of obedience because true obedience is taking to heart what Christ puts before us. This is obedience. Obedience is not carrying out an order. Obedience is learning to love what is before us knowing that maybe it is not our choice but this does not make it unworthy of being taken seriously, is not a reason to refuse to feel responsible for it, take it to heart. This means constantly being open to the unforeseen – what we don't know, but exists.

What could Joseph have wanted for Jesus? He had taught him a trade, taught him how to survive in the world, taught him to pray, taught him to respect his friends. We should not imagine Jesus as the little saint outside of human logic. It is not me saying this but the Gospel: 'And Jesus increased in wisdom and years, and in divine and human favour.' (Lk 2:52).

'To increase' means or implies things happening gradually, all the way through to death. Joseph, along with Mary, properly educated, 'drew out' all the potential of wisdom and grace in Jesus. Jesus had love for his father here on Earth, too. He loved Joseph who put aside his expectations in order to develop the calling of a son who was not his but whom he had decided to take to heart. Things become ours not by ownership but because we take them to heart. We always belong to those who took us to heart. They are the only ones who can use the possessive adjective of us. The one who takes us to heart is also the first to let us go, set us free. Taking to heart is different from filling our heart. Joseph does not use Jesus to fill a void. Joseph loves Jesus by making possible freedom of the kind that allows him to stay behind in Jerusalem, throwing him (Joseph) and Mary in to anguish and anxiety: 'Child, why have you treated us like this? Look your father and I have been searching for you in great anxiety' (Lk 2:48).

When any of us has put our hand to our vocation, a relationship, some project or work, we have had expectations. But remaining Christian, believers like Joseph, means being ready every day to renounce our own expectations, make room for what God has in mind which is always greater, different, more capacious, more inclusive than what we had in mind.

We must learn to yield, but not to be losers. We need to learn to yield like Joseph, and Joseph yields because he takes things to heart. He takes this woman, Mary, to heart, the woman he already loved, but accepts not touching her, and protects her and the child in her womb. At times Joseph's faith surpasses Mary's. He has to trust the word, dreams, adverse circumstances.

I believe that at this moment in history, the Church needs Joseph, the world needs Joseph, that is, people who take things to heart, return once more to the practice of true fatherhood as he did. People who know how to put aside their own expectations and leave room for God's, for God's dreams. People who know that charity and holiness are not to be found in heroic deeds but in the thirty years of hidden life at Nazareth. It is just too simple to die once, heroically. The problem is dying every day for thirty, forty, fifty, eighty years. Every day. Daily martyrdom. Nazareth. The world calls this dailiness 'routine' in a pejorative sense because this is where freedom, emptiness, lack of meaning are experienced. But if Jesus and Mary are there in our everyday, what are we lacking? We have Christ; what is lacking? Nothing is lacking for us to be happy now.

God, who should be the certainty of our life, enters our life and makes himself our Son. Faith is not simply a father watching over us. Faith is a God who becomes a baby and hands himself over to our responsibility. Until we become adults and feel responsible for Christ, not only will we never be like Joseph, but we will not be able to make room for the dream God has for the world, this community, the Church, ourselves. It is only the birth of genuine personal responsibility that in turn gives birth to something new. When I feel an unending responsibility for Christ, a story of salvation always sprouts. We would all like a father who covers our back, but God the Father has chosen to place his Son in our hands. I, who want a father, find a God who makes me a father. In order to educate me to be a son, God makes me a father, makes me a responsible, genuine believer who understands that he has a responsibility for Christ like Joseph did.

Looking after, taking care of.

If we do not look after Christ like Joseph looked after this Son, no wisdom or grace will increase in our life. Indeed, it will die. Had Joseph not protected Jesus, Herod would have murdered him. Yet he protects him without special effects, without spectacular assistance, without magic. He protects him by using his intelligence, prudence, practicality, heart, and even his dreams and fear.

When you become endlessly responsible for what has been given you, then you begin to make room for God's purpose, you defend Christ and Christ is safe. And while Jesus is alive there is always hope. When we fail our responsibility, it is as if we were cutting Christ himself out of our life. It is the mistaken mentality of someone who thinks that God can act without involving any of us. God can do so but does not. We think: 'Even if I do nothing with my responsibility he will do something.' Certainly he will, not here and not with you. God's grace is always in proportion to the growth of our sense of responsibility. I believe this may be the most beautiful message Jesus leaves us for any genuine renewal; the maturing of any change is humble, holy, real increase in my responsibility for Christ.

Epilogue

(Instructions for working miracles)

One day Peter and John were going up to the temple at the hour of prayer, at thee o'clock in the afternoon. And a man lame from birth was being carried in. People would lay him daily at the gate of the temple called the Beautiful Gate so that he could ask for alms from those entering the temple. When he saw Peter and John about to go into the temple, he asked them for alms. Peter looked intently at him, as did John, and said, 'Look at us.' And he fixed his attention on them, expecting to receive something from them. But Peter said, 'I have no silver or gold, but what I have I give you; in the name of Jesus Christ of Nazareth, stand up and walk.' And he took him by the right hand and raised him up; and immediately his feet and ankles were made strong. Jumping up he stood and began to walk, and he entered the temple with them, walking and leaping and praising God. All the people saw him walking and praising God, and they recognised him as the one who used to sit and ask for alms at the Beautiful Gate of the temple; and they were filled with wonder and amazement at what had happened to him (Acts 3:1–10).

I chose this passage from Acts of the Apostles to conclude our reflections and trace out a brief companion handbook for our possible miracles.

We could describe the event narrated as a news item because the Acts of the Apostles is a kind of diary of the first Christian Community. It is apparently a very simple story but in reality is loaded with deeper meaning.

There is a man, a lame man. The first pause we should make is here, with the word 'lame.'

Who is the lame man? He is someone unable to live a normal life due to an illness, a defect, a difficult situation. Obviously the lame man Acts speaks of is marked in his body, has physical problems which stop him from working and looking after himself. But we should broaden the definition of lame to anyone who has something preventing him or her from living a normal life. Sorrow, some concern, a slice of that person's history which they cannot digest. Put briefly, something in life which takes calm normality from us. And because of that we find ourselves having to beg for our living.

This kind of dependence, this existential asking for alms, is an attitude we do not immediately manage to focus on. We spend a lot of time trying to understand it at any depth and accepting it. We are no longer living but begging for life: a little bit of happiness, a little bit of attention from others. The Acts of the Apostles is very precise in saying he was being carried in and laid at the gate. This man could not get there himself. His is the condition of someone who can only live by being a burden. It stops him from making progress, has nailed him there, stopped him. It has made him lacking and taken away the possibility of a normal life, has violated his freedom, put him in a situation of submission, dependence, begging.

But the thing that strikes us most is how accustomed this man is to his circumstances: seeing Peter and John about to enter the Temple, without any particular inspiration he asks them for alms, an offering. Perhaps he did not even look at them or look them in the face. He simply puts out his hand in what is by now an automatic gesture.

It is Peter, instead, who makes a gesture which runs counter to the norm and gives us the clue that comes before any miracle: acknowledgement.

I think we would all have had the experience at some stage of meeting a poor person asking for alms. The more widespread attitude is serene indifference. I pretend the person does not exist. We pretend to be in a hurry, pass by at a distance or look the other way, check our mobile phone, cross the street, act in such a way that our gaze and the beggar's do not connect. Ours is a structured indifference also accompanied by unexceptionable and reasonable motivations. Peter does quite the opposite. He looked intently at him. We avert our gaze so we do not feel awkward, and look elsewhere. Peter does not look elsewhere, but exactly at this man who is invisible to so many.

However, before coming to the very brief dialogue Peter has with him, I would like to bring attention to another detail. We have already seen what it means to be lame, then added the matter of indifference, and then the difference Peter brings by showing interest in him. Let's now for a moment bring our attention to what the text does not say regarding the interpretation of this inconvenience, this lameness, this marginalising condition the man experiences at the Temple gate. The problem is this. So often we want God to interpret our life, provide an explanation for it, as if we were looking for some theory, which makes it automatically bearable.

It says the man was lame from birth. This means there is no plausible reason for saying it is through some fault of his. The explanation cannot go back to something he has done wrong, a consequence of mistaken actions. Why does a child have to undergo the injustice of something like this, of innocent suffering? It is because of this suffering that he now finds himself begging for his living at the feet of passers-by. Why has this happened to him? What took place in his history? Were his parents perhaps to blame? Why so much suffering? Why must he find himself in this situation not of his choice? We ask these things about him because they are questions that concern us all.

None of us goes looking for suffering, for situations that make us lame in some way. But at times it happens anyway that we meet these situations in life. We can be wounded, experience situations we cannot get on top of. Many things happen in life without us choosing them, as we said earlier. But this is only one part of the story because we must also honestly say that sometimes some of the circumstances which ground us, stop us, marginalise us, have come about though our actions. If anything, we should ask ourselves why God allows this. Should not love also protect us from the wrong we could do to ourselves? However, this is not the case for this man. His is innocent suffering, *de facto* suffering. A reality he discovers but does not choose. He has done nothing to deserve this sorrow, yet sorrow it is. It is here that a mistaken use of faith can occur, thinking that there ought be an explanation as to why someone suffers. Even if we were to discover it, what would change in this man's life?

The true miracle does not lie in explanations. If someone were to explain the reason for his or her condition to a person born lame, it might be a reason, but it would not bring about any change in practical terms. Instead, Jesus teaches us something radically different. Perhaps it does not answer all the existential whys and wherefores of our life, but it takes to heart what we are experiencing, takes to heart the fact that we are dependent, that we beg for our living. It changes, not interprets it. The miracle is a change, not an interpretation. While we use faith to interpret our life, we will never change our life. Jesus enters our life to transform it, change it, not to catalogue it. Psychological relief is only a part-time, meagre consolation. Jesus takes the existence of the problem seriously, not its philosophical apparatus. We can storm heaven as to why, with requests for the profound reasons for things that happen to us, as if we could grasp it all, embrace the entire horizon in an instant. In reality, what we manage to see is only a very limited part of things. We do not see the complete picture. God takes us seriously in the fragment we are experiencing, in the slice of effort which often has the after-taste of mystery.

Yet, resolving the problem is not freeing us from it, but from its consequences: the consequences which have taken our freedom from us, put us in the situation of begging for a living. Our story, our malformations, our warping and twisting do not horrify God. Perhaps it is we who accept them. Our diversity is always something we experience in a problematic way. The problem is not that the man cannot walk, but the consequences of not being able to walk, which make the man so totally crushed by his existence. The first miracle, the first way for him to encounter Jesus Christ, is not through healing but through another man like him who is interested in him, his story.

Peter does this. A Christian is first of all someone interested in others not someone who interprets others and their lives. The Christian is not someone who gives explanations to others, and above all is not someone who just passes by. Christians do not use indifference to advance, so that they do not soil their hands. A true Christian always works miracles, the miracles of difference, looking someone in the eye, acknowledging them.

If there are people in our life, it is never by accident. Indifference cannot be the measure of our lives. Every true miracle passes through the difference of showing interest. This is Peter: 'Peter looked intently at him, as did John, and said, "Look at us."' These are beautiful words, words that accomplish miracles. 'Look me in the eye.' At that moment it is as if Peter himself were giving back lost dignity to the man. By saying 'Look at us' it is as if we were wanting to say: 'I have recognised that you are not just an extended hand. You don't coincide with your poverty. You too are a man like me! Look at my face. Look me in the eye!'

We are unable to give something to all the people we meet in our lives, but looking intently at them and reminding ourselves they are people is the least Christianity we can give them. It is reminding ourselves that behind the limitations, behind the ugliness of one or other kind is hidden the human being with dignity. The poverty and ugliness sometimes cover over so much goodness that we fail to recognise the humanity beneath. We note the stink, the filth, We note the fact that they are horrible to look at and to have near us. But we do not recognise that all the reliquary of rags, filth, hides a human being. Peter does though: Look me in the eye because I have recognised who you are behind your misery. You do not coincide with that misery. You are someone much greater.

'And he fixed his attention on them, expecting to receive something from them. But Peter said, "I have no silver or gold, but what I have I give you; in the name of Jesus of Nazareth, stand up and walk." '

I want to pause at the heart of this passage, right at this sentence, to understand something truly important: very often we confuse Christianity with philanthropy. We think that to be Christian means only going to a soup kitchen for the poor and giving a hand, or some act of kindness to a sick or elderly person. In all this activity of charity we think we have exhausted Christianity. The truth is that there is no need to be Christian to go to a poor person and offer him or her something to eat. Christians have no monopoly on this. There are many good people who do not recognise Jesus as the Son of God, do not even believe in God, but do so much good for others in this way. Maybe they go through life feeding the hungry, looking after people, helping. What we have in addition is not silver and gold, not something simply material to give. The more we have is to be involved with the person, not only the poverty. It is knowing how to acknowledge the whole person, not only their needs. Peter says: 'I have no money but I do have something precious: In the name of Jesus Christ get up and walk.'

Here is what will change everything. This man who walks again represents someone who regains life. It is as if he were completely regaining the freedom he lacked. He is no longer in a position of having to beg for a living. He is once more the key player in his own story. This is the change Peter gives him by handing him over to Christ. He does not simply offer him aid but gives him the root of his lost freedom. The miracle is not so much that his feet have straightened out and he begins to walk but the fact that he once again assumes a position of freedom with regard to everything around him.

Christ takes the determinism from us that was holding us in its grip. He gives us back the grace of no longer needing to beg for our living despite it being manifested in fragility and weakness. Christ gives us back the memory of our dignity as human beings. He returns us to being human even when life pushes us into the corner, stops us entering, or leaves us at the door.

The encounter with Christ reconciles us with what, up until yesterday, was our desperation. It is a miracle that so often is not seen by others. It is something one discovers in first person simply because one is no longer crushed, oppressed, but back to the living again, even with twisted feet, even though externally the problem may still hold its grip on one. Sometimes we can be freer this way than many others who perhaps simply have a formal freedom, outer movement, but nothing of substance.

This is Christianity, Christianity is not the management of a problem, but the substantial solution to the problem. Christianity is not managing but taking to heart. It is seeking to bring this freedom wherever, despite the problems, needs, fragility.

If it were only a question of form, our God would be an unjust God. The problem is not form but the substance of our own life and the freedom that allows us to feel that. The true Christian miracle lies not in sensationalism but in the slow, silent and at times hidden work of the liberation of individuals. Effective and hidden. Thus the Christian miracle makes room in the world.

If you want to work a miracle, acknowledge people.

If you want to work a miracle do not simply give what you have in your pockets but offer Christ. Offer people meaningful relationships. Let Christ become flesh in your gestures: you will see it is him, because the person before you will begin to feel freer than when he or she first met you.

Perhaps you cannot remove someone's pain or sorrow, but if Jesus becomes part of it, it is no longer cause for desperation. We need to take Christ's hand so he can come to the people we encounter: 'And he took him by the right hand and raised him up.' How beautiful the gesture is also when it is described by the Word of God. One could get involved by standing at a distance and maybe shouting: 'In the name of Jesus get up and walk!' Without touching. But Peter touches him because charity is always a practical, concrete thing. It is the miracle of incarnate Love.

We can confuse charity with emotion. We think that since we are moved by pain we are also automatically charitable. This way we misunderstand charity because it is not merely being moved.

Charity is work, concreteness. Peter touches the man, becomes his neighbour, does something for him. We do not need to feel good, but we must be so, be good, in deed. Charity is always active to the core which is why Peter takes him by the right hand. It is the miracle of deeds. The prime matter for miracles is our humanity made available.

> 'All the people saw him walking and praising God,
> and they recognised him as the one who used to sit and

> ask for alms at the Beautiful Gate of the temple; and they were filled with wonder and amazement at what had happened to him.'

This man himself became a proclamation. He is not only a miracle but a witness. He himself became a deed that speaks the truth of encounter with Christ.

Faith is not a little bit of honey in our mouth, making it easier to swallow a bitter pill. At times it is something that stings, like salt on an open wound. But it is precisely because of this that it prevents things from going bad.

We are called to be salt, not honey.